THE
YEAR
THE
QUEEN
DIED

A Media Diary of 2022 with

DAVID J A HALLAM

PublishU Ltd

www.PublishU.com

ISBN: 9798387385858

**Dedicated to the five lovely friends
who died in 2022:**

Leslie Clayden

Albert Holmes

John Anderson

Janet Rowan

Jackie Atkin

Contents

Preface: David Hallam introduces his TV reviews of 2022   11

2022: The year we kept calm and carried on   15

Radio's Room 5 beats the blockbusters   19

Cooking bonanza, fake psychics and a scenic river   23

A mixed bag as BBC3 returns   27

The brutal truth about hospital life   31

Ant, Dec, Boy Erased and the Archbishop   35

A debt of gratitude to the war correspondents   39

I slept on the sofa for Mary Whitehouse   43

Ritualised abuse in plain sight on our TV screens   47

How The Ritz and a holiday camp have a message for Methodists   51

The trauma faced by victims of war and survivors of rape   55

Cadbury "exposed" is a bit like being bitten by the Easter Bunny   59

The pain and joy of family connections   63

Breast cancer, menopause and a spiky woman police officer   67

There is more to buying an electric car than a green preen — 71

Let's have some luvly Jubbly for the Jubilee knees up! — 75

Hunting witches, abusing MPs and even Private Godfrey faces abuse — 79

The hope and optimism of the Coronation and Coventry Cathedral — 83

OMG! Love Island returns—but who benefits? — 87

Cor! Wotta scorcher! Hot summers and the Methodist who started the Glastonbury Festival — 91

Guinness takes the spirit out, but the Baptists keep it in — 95

When Jagger was banned — 99

"I'm a romantic, sentimental, traditional Anglican" Meet TV broadcaster, former MP and teddy bear collector Gyles Brandreth — 103

Goodbye Neighbours, hello Newsreader — 109

Brum's 'Golden Decade' starts with the Commonwealth Games — 113

The Indian Summer of freedom, violence, hate and hope — 117

Social media: the life raft and the ship wreck — 121

Diana was pursued by the media in both life and death — 125

As the nights draw in, the coppers are looking for the villains — 129

"Nana" tells us all we need to know with the death of our Queen — 133

"Strictly" is back, but have ITV already thrown in the towel for Saturday night ratings? — 137

Ten days when time stood still as we mourned our Queen — 141

Time for a little sauce and lots of sparkle — 145

How self-esteem and music make for good mental health and well-being — 149

Fifty years of Radio 4's 'Thought for the day' — 153

The surprises and challenges of Black history — 157

We have more choice, but after 100 years the BBC reigns supreme — 161

Behind the scenes at 'Strictly' with a former Home Secretary — 165

Ram Gidoomal – the refugee who came to know Jesus — 169

TV cooking competitions in the age of the food bank — 173

After such an horrific history, Jews don't count — 177

History is never about the past, and what about those Christmas ads? — 181

Gyles Brandreth Elizabeth: An Intimate Portrait   185

There's not much on the telly, let's see what's   189
on the wireless'

Harry Taylor Victor Grayson: In search of Britain's Lost   193
Revolutionary

The wicked "contract" that is destroying our   195
Royal Family

Index of Reviews   201

About the Author   211

Other Publications   213

THE YEAR THE QUEEN DIED

DAVID J A HALLAM

Preface
David Hallam introduces
his TV reviews of 2022

During 2022, I was asked to contribute a weekly TV and radio column to the Methodist Recorder, the world's leading Methodist newspaper. I had already contributed to the column for a few weeks in 2021 and was pleased to be asked to take over permanently from February 2022.

As I watched, listened and wrote each week, I became aware that many of the programmes we reviewed were actually previews for those who would watch on the various catch-up and streaming services—either on their TV set, home computer, laptop or mobile. I wanted to make the column as useful as possible to those who would catch up later. Collecting the reviews for this book will make it easier for those who want to catch up beyond the shelf life of a weekly newspaper.

From the start, I set myself some guidelines:

Firstly, with just one exception, which I explain in the review, I wanted to only include free-to-view material. It isn't the purpose of this column to promote the various subscription services, and there is easily enough entertainment, information, and challenge on terrestrial TV and radio, the various podcast and YouTube channels, and on the catch-up services.

Secondly, there needed to be a mix between very popular programmes on prime time and the more niche productions that may appeal to a faith based audience, particularly—but not exclusively—Christian. Where I found programmes that may be of help to people working in several fields, such as bereavement or youth work, that was a bonus.

Thirdly, the production schedules of a weekly newspaper mean it is impossible to offer reviews of moving events, such as a big sports competition or a political crisis, except in the most general terms.

In this book, I have also included a fascinating interview with a well-known TV personality and the reviews of several books, which I contributed to the Methodist Recorder during 2022.

I'd like to take this opportunity to thank the staff of the **Methodist Recorder** for their encouragement and support during the year, and also to my wife Claire, who very patiently reads my articles before submission, correcting my English and sometimes giving me helpful guidance.

I hope you enjoy reading these reviews, as much as I enjoyed writing them.

David Hallam
Smethwick

How to catch-up

BBC television programmes – BBC iPlayer &
www.bbc.co.uk/iplayer
(you will be asked if you have a TV licence)*

BBC radio programmes – BBC Sounds and
www.bbc.co.uk/sounds

ITV programmes – ITVX and www.ITV.com*

Channel 4 – ALL4 and www.channel4.com*

Channel 5 – MY5 and www.channel5.com*

Dave, Drama, W and Yesterday – UKTV PLAY and
www.uktvplay.co.uk*

*Source: *Radio Times*

DAVID J A HALLAM

2022

The year we Kept Calm and Carried On

The war in Ukraine, turmoil in government, inflation, strikes and the death of our beloved Queen Elizabeth II have meant that many of the great TV and radio events of 2022 have been on our news and current affairs programmes. This was the year we had to keep calm and carry on, as did our broadcasters.

The planned schedules have played their part, especially with events like the Platinum Jubilee, that no one alive today will ever see again. But, too often, reality has blocked out the fiction that makes up much of our entertainment.

Who will ever forget the bravery of those reporters and camera operators who stayed in Kyiv during February and March, facing another cynical use of the Red Army tanks by Vladimir Putin? In the first days of the war, it looked as though the Russians would sweep to victory because the Ukrainians would simply fold. Visions of darkened streets, massive fireballs, women and children fleeing for their lives all conspired to help us understand the reality of war.

We will never again hear Her Majesty give her Christmas Day message. Each year she said more about her faith, which was clearly very important to her. The Platinum Jubilee celebrations on our television in June seemed muted as if we all knew what was coming and, in September, it did. On the day of her death, our TV stations brought us the sad news as it unfolded. Hasty decisions were made to rejig the schedules and many of the special programmes seemed a re-run of those that had celebrated the Jubilee just fourteen weeks before.

The very last pictures of the Queen on our screens were of those when she said goodbye to Boris Johnson and welcomed Liz Truss as Prime Minister. The political turmoil in government was carefully recorded and the hustings between Rishi Sunak and Liz Truss struggled to grip viewers' attention. After a year of turmoil at the top, we now have a government which seems remote and incompetent. Television and radio are supposed to be "balanced" but that sometimes gets reduced to timidity.

Normally, the big sports occasions grace the summer schedules where they really belong. We expect tense matches from Wimbledon to be played into the evening. This year, we also had the joy of seeing the Commonwealth Games unfold in Birmingham and the whole country seemed to get behind these sportsmen and women. Who cared if the scheduled programmes were shuffled aside? But football's World Cup Competition from Quatar shattered the late autumn schedules and felt intrusive. On these dark and cold evenings, many of us want to be settled around the TV with a cocoa and relax with a familiar programme.

The re-arrival of BBC3 as a terrestrial channel, promised great things, but seems to have got into something of a rut. GB News and Times Radio had hoped for a bigger audience in 2022, but both seemed lost in the ghetto inhabited by political anoraks. TalkTV was launched in April, but has yet to be seen by anyone else I know.

Anniversaries have been a major part of the schedules and none more so than the celebration of the launching of the BBC in 1922. Lots of good archive footage and an opportunity to see some favourite episodes of BBC programmes, especially sitcoms, that are rarely aired today. They are now often accompanied by warnings of inappropriate language and attitudes. Surely one of broadcasting's innovations in 2022?

The 40th anniversary of the launch of Channel 4 seemed altogether less flamboyant. I remember sitting with colleagues at our advertising agency watching the first evening's shows, discussing whether we should divert advertising to the new channel (we didn't).

Other anniversaries reminded us of past sorrows. The 40th anniversary of the Falklands conflict may have been expected to create more programmes, but it felt very subdued. Perhaps the schedulers saw the future 50th anniversary as being more significant? Sadly, many of those who took part in those battles will not be with us in ten years' time.

The 25th anniversary of the death of Princess Diana brought us programmes which commemorated that short life and those dramatic days. It is all the more poignant as we see the stresses between the two brothers, William and Harry, being played out on our screens.

It was the 75th anniversary of the dramatic unwinding of "British" India that bought us some first-class, and moving, documentaries on both television and radio. Many of us have friends and neighbours from multiple communities in the Indian sub-continent and this was an opportunity to revisit some of the issues which can tear those neighbours apart.

Having watched TV on behalf of the **Methodist Recorder** for the best part of a year, I would make just one observation: Why on earth does so much television have to be reduced to the "reality" format? It works for "Strictly" and for some talent shows, but sewing and cooking?

Meanwhile in all the turmoil, my admiration for BBC radio continues to grow. They really kept calm and carried on.

Methodist Recorder, 23rd December, 2022

Radio 4's Room 5
beats the blockbusters

In January we saw the launch or return of expensive television blockbusters featuring gritty police officers, the secret world of plants, midwives, faraway hospitals, and even, yet again, the Kray gangsters.

But "**Room 5**" (Radio 4) beats the lot. Journalist Helen Merriman introduces six ordinary people who faced a diagnosis that changed everything.

Serena was seventeen weeks pregnant. Already a mother of two children, she had become used to the idea that there would be a latecomer to the family home. However, the doctors explained her options. She could take a tablet now and she would miscarry. If she left it another five weeks, a needle would be put into her stomach and then into the baby's heart so that it would die.

Serena had been called into see the consultant after a scan, underwent further tests and was told that the child had Patau's Syndrome. The NHS website explains that it is "serious rare genetic disorder caused by having an additional copy of chromosome 13 in some or all of the body's cells. It's also called trisomy 13".

The chances of Serena's baby going full term and living for even a few hours after birth were slim. Even if the baby survived, it would have multiple handicaps ranging from additional digits on the hands and feet through to serious mobility and learning difficulties. Serena's story is still available on BBC Sounds, so you can find out for yourself which heart-breaking option she chose.

Like me, Jay Blades of "The Repair Shop" is a Hackney lad. In our day, schools in Hackney struggled. I can't do simple arithmetic, Jay never learnt to read. After a successful business career and becoming a charismatic TV presenter, he decided it was time he learnt to read— and he made a documentary about his progress. **"Learning to Read at 51"** (BBC1) tells Jay's story, but also that of thousands who can't read, many of whom we come across on the fringes of our congregations or in chaplaincy work. Jay showed that there are resources available to help people catch up. This programme in itself may be a very useful pastoral tool to encourage those we know who would like to follow Jay's example.

So let's look at the peak time blockbusters. Hackney is a short bus ride to Poplar, so I take more than a passing interest in **"Call the Midwife"** (BBC1) now in its eleventh series. In many ways, it's a brilliant production, really capturing the material culture of the 1950s and 60s with the clothing, hair styles and furnishings. I even feel that I knew some of the characters as a child. But many of the plot lines, and there are always three or four in every episode, verge on being emotionally abusive, the more so as the series moves from Jennifer Worth's original stories set in the 1950s. It may be that, for me, it's literally too close to home, but not comfortable viewing on a Sunday evening.

"The Good Karma Hospital" (ITV 1) offers a slightly easier-to-watch alternative, but still manages to tug the heart strings. Dr Ruby Walker, played by Amrita Acharia, joined the "GKH" in India, way back in 2017, being disillusioned with our NHS, and I suspect broken hearted. Now in the fifth year of her exile, she is still unable to find love. However, the story really revolves around the hospital director, Dr Lydia Fonseca, played by Amanda Redman, who has developed something of a niche portraying confident women able to dominate inadequate men, one of whom is portrayed by Neil Morrisey from the notorious "Men Behaving Badly" TV series.

A contemporary theme arrived in the first episode, when Ruby makes a home visit to a young girl with a highly infectious disease. This leads to a lockdown and quarantine for Ruby with a doctor from a neighbouring hospital—Samir, who is "fresh off the boat" from the UK and has much to learn. Perhaps Ruby will be the one to teach him?

There are two new "gritty" police drama series. "**The Responder**" (BBC1) follows the night shifts of Chris Carson, played by Martin Freeman, who responds to urgent calls, never knowing where he will be next or what he will deal with. We were treated to an apparently unsupervised lone policeman roaming Liverpool in a disjointed selection of cameos. These were interspersed by flashbacks to counselling sessions, snapshots of a problematic home life and colleagues telling him to pull himself together. In light of recent crimes involving maverick police officers, it was hardly reassuring. I didn't watch the second episode.

"**Trigger Point**" (ITV 1) features a Metropolitan Police bomb disposal team. We learnt that they were veterans of our war in Afghanistan. Consisting of two black men and a young white woman, they were as far away from the stiff-upper-lipped middle class boffins who are normally portrayed as bomb disposal experts. Their first job was to tackle a terrorist incident on a housing estate where the locals were very unfriendly. A fake bomb was followed by finding a kidnaped man wearing an explosive vest. He was used as bait for a more serious explosion. Vicky McClure, previously in "Line of Duty" is superb as the lead actor and this series will have us on the edge of our seats.

Methodist Recorder, 4th February, 2022

Cooking bonanza
- fake psychics and a scenic river

For those who enjoy cooking programmes, the last few weeks have been something of a bonanza. There's also been a very meaty contribution to those who counsel bereaved people tempted by spiritualism. And there's a wonderfully relaxing programme to start the weekend.

Chef Jamie Oliver is back as the host of the fifth series of **"The Great Cookbook Challenge"** (C4). It's a collaboration between a publisher, the broadcaster and lots of aspiring cook book authors. Each week, six aspiring authors make a dish from their proposed cook book and then pitch the sample and the concept to a panel of cookery experts and a publisher. Two go through to a future round and, eventually, one is declared a winner with the prize of a book contract with a major publisher.

The first episode showed just how far we are moving from the "meat and two veg" regime of the last century. The first contestant was a surgeon who had a thing about bread, which I must admit I didn't quite grasp. The prospective author of "The Green Greek" created a vegetarian risotto, a great title, but the dish looked very plain. I was impressed with the contestant who produced a rabbit dish that was aimed at recovering vegetarians. The publisher refused point blank to have a taste. My favourite—who I will tip as the eventual winner—was a cheeky young man called Callum, who managed to make vegan food seem easy to prepare and tasty.

I had great hopes of learning how to cook Michelin star food from the second series of "**Simply Raymond Blanc**" (ITV1). The word "simply" was the attraction. Alas, most of the meals were simple if you have a well-stocked, well-equipped kitchen with its own garden. His cheese on toast, called a "croque madame", was unbelievably complicated. But Raymond redeemed himself with his last dish: he demonstrated how to make a great omelette. I've been using the wrong mix, wrong pan, and wrong spatula since 1963. In fact, I've just enjoyed one for lunch.

Talking about food, calling Padstow Methodist Church! Would you nip down the road and tell Padstow's most famous restauranteur how to prepare vegetables for a pasty? My Cornish diaspora wife normally enjoys "**Rick Stein's Cornwall**" (BBC1) but dicing, rather than slicing vegetables, as Rick did, is a major culinary crime, according to the best pasty cook in Smethwick.

Sadly, we all have to manage our grief when someone close to us dies. There are always unfinished conversations and questions which we long to have resolved. Scripture makes it clear that Christians should not attempt to contact the dead, and that it can be very dangerous to attempt to do so. "**Fake Psychic**" (Radio 4) tells the story of how bereaved people were exploited by unscrupulous "spiritualists" in the 1950s and 1960s

Larner Keene, self-ordained as a "Reverend", made a fortune by tricking people into believing he could channel the voices of loved ones from beyond the grave. His tricks, and those of other psychics were deceptively simple. They would harvest gossip and information about their adherents and then pretend that they had received a message from their spirit guide. They even created a filing system on their victims which they would share with other psychics.

If Keene didn't know a congregation, he would gather information by asking for prayer requests in sealed envelopes. He would pretend to be able to read the contents of each request whilst they were still sealed. In reality it was a piece of simple conjuring.

Keene eventually repented of his crimes and even wrote a book denouncing spiritualism. In later life he contracted AIDS and became a very effective campaigner. If only his gifts had been used as productively for the early part of his life as they were towards the end

Those of us involved in pastoral care should be aware that there are still people who will see bereavement as an opportunity for exploitation. Closer to home we should be aware that similar trickery can sometimes be used to create "words of knowledge" which mislead and abuse vulnerable people. Churches need to incorporate an understanding of these dangers into our safeguarding, but also equip ourselves to test the spirits.

Thank you to Rev Andy Fishburne, our Connexional Discipleship and Faith Formation Officer for leading an inspiring "**Daily Service**" (Radio 4) focused on Christian Unity.

"The World's Most Scenic Rivers" (Channel 5) is back! Going out early Friday evening, it is the ideal wind down after a busy week and a great refuge on catch-up. The first episode of the second series travelled the River Bure, which feeds the Broads in Norfolk. The river may be scenic now but at one point it was a hub of industry and a major transport route. The history is carefully told with lovely clear descriptions as we follow the different periods from monastic peat production, which incidentally created the Broads, through to intensive agriculture and the eventual emergence as a very important holiday destination. Every local who spoke, appreciated how blessed they were to live and work there. It was expertly narrated by Bill Nighy without an intrusive celebrity presenter hogging the limelight. Let's hope they don't run out of scenic rivers and that it runs for many years to come.

Methodist Recorder, 11th February, 2022

A Mixed Bag
as BBC3 returns

BBC3 is back on terrestrial television after a gap of six years. Launched in 2003, the channel was intended to capture the elusive 18-34 demographic. In 2016, it was taken off terrestrial and placed online as a streaming service. Once again, BBC3 is a mixed bag: the channel that produced the heart-warming "Gavin and Stacey" also gave us the unlamented, and now disowned, "Little Britain".

The first weeks of BBC3 on terrestrial have been dominated by sport: first football's Africa Cup, and then by the Winter Olympics. **"Freeze: Skating on the Edge"** (BBC3) followed the young people who form the GB figure skating team. They may look glamorous as they effortlessly glide across the ice, but this series shows the pain, challenges and heartbreaks that proceed their selection. Preparation for this year's Winter Olympics has been compromised by the pandemic, with the skaters practising their moves in local parks and on roller skates. The men have to be especially fit in order to lift their partners. The women have to be brave enough to know that at any moment they could fall seven feet onto the ice. And well done anyone who can manage the "triple axel" without falling!

BBC3's flagship entertainment programme is appropriately placed well beyond the nine o'clock watershed. But I really don't see it appealing to their target audience of young adults. One of the performers promised, "We are taking you to weird and wonderful places," and **"RuPaul's**

Drag Race: UK vs the World" (BBC3) certainly does! RuPaul was a successful drag queen who created a reality contest for a US TV channel in 2009. Since then, the format has been franchised across the world, including BBC3.

It is intended as entertainment and some of the costumes, dancing and singing are creative and professional. However, a lot of the banter is crude and the constant exclamation, "Oh My God!" is clearly misplaced. The contestants laughed a lot, sometimes as if they were excited schoolgirls, although in truth there wasn't much for the viewer to laugh with or at.

As society, at last, begins to understand that both transpeople and women should expect to be portrayed with respect, men creating an exaggerated caricature of femininity already seems outdated and verges on the offensive. In a few years' time this programme will be treated with the same sort of embarrassment we now regard the "Black and White Minstrel Show". You don't find that on iPlayer!

I was intrigued by the announcement at the start of Her Majesty's Platinum Jubilee Year that the Duchess of Cornwall will be styled "Queen Consort" in the event of Prince Charles ascending to the throne. I am wondering if an abdication is on the cards—which made **"The Queen: 70 Glorious Years"** (BBC1) seem even more poignant. We have been well served by a head of state who has experienced so much. This programme showcased the changes that have happened in those seventy years. For many of her subjects, not every year was glorious, and the programme acknowledges that. There will be more retrospection in coming months but this has already set a high standard.

Methodism has always had a difficult relationship with alcohol. It is a myth that temperance was a condition of membership. My own church was split in the 1920s as one faction implied that only teetotallers could be Christians. On a recent episode of **"In Our Time"** (BBC Radio 4) we learnt "the pledge" to abstain from alcohol was signed by seven men in 1832. The movement spread rapidly throughout working class urban communities. Temperance halls became a regular feature of Victorian civic society. It was instructive to hear how society dealt with alcohol during the nineteenth century.

The 1820s were a time of complete deregulation and "gin palaces" could be found in every community. Then came changes in the law to achieve some regulation and promote beer, which was seen as less dangerous. This was followed by the campaigns for temperance, though interestingly they stopped short of a call for prohibition. Every now and then the contributors made references to our current drug problems. This begs the question as to whether there is anything modern Britain could learn from the Victorian solutions.

A more recent difficulty for Methodism has been the decision to conduct same-sex weddings. For Jason and Ben, both trainee presbyters at Queen's College in Birmingham, the outcome of the 2021 conference has been critical as they plan their wedding. On **"Episode 75: LGBT+ History Month 2022"** (The Methodist Podcast) they speak about their reaction to the decision, the hurts, the tears and the joy. Both were very positive about the way in which Connexion discussed the issue, though they were fearful of the outcome at the time. They get married in June and hope to be stationed together. We can be sure we will hear more from Jason and Ben as they continue their journey.

I was only able to hear the first scheduled episode of **"Book of the Week: On Consolation"** (Radio 4) based on Michael Ignatieff's new book exploring the language of consolation in history, literature, philosophy and art. His impressive perspective on the book of Job and the Psalms has certainly persuaded me that the whole series is worth hearing on catch up, or even buying the book.

Methodist Recorder, 18th February, 2022

The Brutal Truth
about Hospital life

It is appropriate that the rooms set aside for operations in hospital are called "theatres". Every operation comes with a narrative and hopefully a happy ending. **"This is Going to Hurt"** (BBC1) is a brutal portrayal of what goes on behind the scenes of many hospital theatres: overworked doctors, strained working relationships, an understanding that sometimes it doesn't pay to be entirely truthful and a reminder that we all have private lives, which are often complicated by the pressures of work. The series is based on a book by former medic, Adam Kay, following his experiences in the National Health Service. Since then, health budgets have tightened, we have lost a lot of good EU medical staff and, of course we've had Covid.

According to Kay, the NHS was near to collapse in 2006, so goodness knows what it must be like now. Ben Wilshaw plays Adam, the obstetrics and gynaecology registrar. He brilliantly manages to balance the serious moments of tragedy contrasting with great humour. His colleague, a junior doctor called Shruti, played by Ambika Mod, absolutely shines as a foil to Adam's sometimes manic behaviour.

Right from the very first news of the murder of teenager Billie-Jo in Hastings in 1997, her case attracted an unusual degree of public interest. Billie-Jo, a foster child, had been bludgeoned to death with a heavy metal tent-peg as she painted a door one Saturday afternoon. The Jenkins were committed Christians. I remember a group of witches even gathered outside the family home and chanted incantations for the murderer to be caught. Sion Jenkins, the foster father, was a deputy head teacher at a local secondary school, a pillar of the community. **"Who killed Billie-Jo"** (Channel 5) is the third full-blown TV documentary to trace the decision by detectives to suspect, then charge, Sion Jenkins with murder. A massaged CV and dubious forensic evidence were critical. Other lines of enquiry were promptly dropped once the police had made up their minds. A familiar story to anyone who has campaigned against a miscarriage of justice.

Sion Jenkins spent six years in prison before the Court of Appeal ordered a retrial, of which there were two, both without a conclusion, leaving Sion Jenkins in legal limbo to this day. Did no one check the tent peg, found at the scene, for fingerprints? Meanwhile, neither Billie-Jo nor Sion Jenkins have the justice they deserve. My gut feeling is that the killer is still at large.

"Louis Theroux's Forbidden America" (BBC2) takes us to the grimmer corners of the US's political spectrum. He introduces us to some very young people who are using the internet to promote views that are clearly offensive. They don't like Jews, black people, gay men and merely tolerate women. One of the rabble-rousers, Nick Fuentes, aged just 22, claimed to make $4000 a day as he spews out his obsessions from his parents' basement. Another got very upset when he was accused of giving a Nazi salute. They all seemed very thin-skinned; the one thing they didn't like, was being called "white nationalists". Let's hope these people stay on the fringes and we don't get any British copycats.

General De Gaulle is quoted by journalist Ceri Thomas in **"Nazarnin"** (Radio 4) as saying, "the state is the coldest of cold monsters". This sad series shows just how cold and monstrous both the British and Iranian governments can be, as Nazarnin Zaghari-Ratcliffe remains imprisoned in Tehran. She was arrested as she was about to leave Iran in 2016. Since then, she has effectively been a hostage because the British government owes Iran millions for a dodgy arms deal. This should be on mainstream TV at peak-time.

In case you think this week's review features too many dark programmes, you can be assured of a lovely piece of escapism with the return of **"Wondrous Wales"** (Channel 4). Focused on rural Wales, we meet hill farmers, lobster fishermen, railway enthusiasts and castle restorers.

The Six Nations rugby festival reminds us the UK has three-and-a-quarter national anthems ("God Save the Queen", "Flower of Scotland", "Hen Wlad Fy Nhadau" and "Ireland's Call"). Sadly, England doesn't have an anthem of its own. The rather mystical "Jerusalem" by William Blake would probably be the popular choice.

"William Blake Singing for England – Omnibus" (BBC4) tells us a lot more about the challenges Blake faced as he created his art whilst earning a living. Largely overlooked by the art establishment at the time, he believed his mission was to depict and protect England's soul, which to him was clearly radical. The programme was first broadcast in 2000 and is available on iPlayer for another fortnight.

I'm sure other readers were envious when they read that Local Preacher Robert Jackson was working on his 46th book (**Methodist Recorder**, 11th February, 2022). Many of us feel we have a book inside us, but how do we get started? In her latest podcast, "**Do you want to write a book?"** (www.bondfieldmarketing.co.uk) Jenny Proctor seeks the help of ghost writer Ginny Carter. Aimed at introverted business people, Jenny and Ginny point out the commercial and professional benefits of being a published author. Most of the points made would be just as applicable to church and faith settings. So, if you want to catch up with Robert, listen in!

Methodist Recorder, 25th February, 2022

Ant, Dec, Boy Erased
and the Archbishop

What better way to relax on a chilly spring weekend evening than to get a KFC bucket with a bottle of pop and sit with the children or grandchildren to enjoy **"Ant and Dec's Saturday Night Takeaway"** (ITV1)? The Geordie duo put together a fast-paced entertainment feast of good clean fun that reaches out to all ages.

The programme is live, which gives it an extra edge. Outside broadcasts come from at least three other locations, ranging from a surprise wedding to an apparently random person finding a lot of money at the end of a "Takeaway Rainbow"—in Rotherham of all places!

The wedding was probably the most audacious thread. Vicky was pulled out of the studio audience after a spa day with her friends. The Covid restrictions had messed up her wedding plans and the couple had lost £28,000 when the venue went bust. Ant and Dec introduced her fiancé on a large screen, complete with family and friends. Forty-five minutes later, following a wild dash in a helicopter and white Roller, much to Vick's surprise, they were officially married.

Just one word of warning: Ant and Dec are sponsored by the National Lottery, which probably explains the lavish production, but means forced-fed pro-gambling propaganda, so that's when you put the kettle on.

"Boy Erased" (BBC3) is neither entertaining, nor enjoyable, but for Christians, compulsive viewing. Based on a true story, it tells what happened when deeply religious parents in Arkansas, played by Russel Crowe and Nicole Kidman, were told that their only teenage son, Jared, played by Lucas Hedges, is a homosexual.

Following conversations with other church leaders, the father insists his son enrol for "conversion therapy" at the creepily-named "Love In Action" camp. His therapy is overseen by Victor Sykes, played by Joel Edgerton, the film's director, who himself, it turns out, is unsuccessfully trying to suppress his own sexuality.

Unregulated, untrained and unaccountable, the therapy focused on group confession and the creation of manliness or femininity. One young woman was forced to provide intimate physical details of her activity with another woman. A young man attended a mock funeral for his masculinity, complete with coffin and candles, and members of his own family, including a pre-teen sister, beating him with a Bible. Unsurprisingly, the Scriptures, prayer and the Holy Spirit, were barely mentioned nor, for that matter, love.

The doings of evangelicals in Arkansas may feel a long way off, but this film has contemporary relevance as the government considers a ban on conversion therapy in the UK. There are concerns that prayer and pastoral conversations would be impossible. Having been involved with various parts of the Christian church in this country for over half a century, I've seen half-baked abusive counselling and so-called "clinical theology" sometimes in Methodist settings. This film shows how easy it is to go wrong, but leaves a lot of other questions unanswered. It's on iPlayer for another fortnight.

Justin Welby, the Archbishop of Canterbury, has taken a brave step into the media with a series of six interviews with other public figures. After hearing the first, with British-Turkish author Elif Shafak, the title of the series, **"The Archbishop Interviews"** (Radio 4) seemed entirely wrong. It was clearly an open-ended conversation and we learnt as much about the Archbishop as we did about Ms Shafak. This is frustrating because both participants raised issues which would have invited further exploration by an experienced interviewer.

Elif Shafak has clearly had an interesting life and described the influence of her grandmother's spirituality, her reconciliation with her father and her dual interest in both faith and doubt. Her most interesting insights were about the hate she received when it became known she identified as bi-sexual. Even then, she felt the love of those who sent her messages of support, and helped her manage her "inner garden".

Other interviewees will be the former Prime Minister Tony Blair; the author Stephen King; the chief executive of Citizens Advice, Clare Moriarty; the former Chief of the Defence Staff, General Sir Nick Carter; and the psychologist Dr Susan Blackmore. The programme goes out at 1:30 pm on Sundays and on BBC Sounds.

"Book of the Week: Metaphysical Animals" (Radio 4) is another real treat which looks at how four women transformed moral philosophy from the despair and confusion of the Second World War. Circumstances meant that, as undergraduates at Somerville College Oxford, Iris Murdoch, Mary Midgley, Philippa Foot and Elizabeth Anscombe were taught by a medley of conscientious objectors, refugees and women who were not conscripted for the war effort. With the justification of mass murders at Hiroshima and Nagasaki, they resolved that moral philosophy must start from scratch and laid the foundation of today's ethical thinking. Brilliantly written by Clare MacCumhaill and Rachel Wiseman, and sensitively read by Fenella Woolgar, it evokes a past era of intellectual challenge that seems missing today. It's only on BBC Sounds for another fourteen days.

Last week, we featured a podcast that encouraged listeners to write that book inside them. This week we go one better with an entire one-hour TV programme devoted to **"How to Write a Mills and Boon"** (BBC4). Stella Duffy has written sixteen novels and thought she would try to capture the special essence. Like many before her, she found it an unexpected challenge. But don't let that put you off having a go!

Methodist Recorder, 4th March, 2022.

A Debt of Gratitude
to the war correspondents

Ever since the Russian army marched into Ukraine, all our attention has been focused on the news from Kyiv. Television and news bulletins have been extended, social media has been consumed with excited chatter and many of us have wept as we have seen the real-life tragedy of people fleeing the violence or seeking shelter.

The Light Brigade was slaughtered in the Crimea on 25th October, 1854. It took a full eighteen days for reports of that battle to make the British press. Now, such a catastrophe would be public knowledge in the UK in just eighteen minutes, we may even see it broadcast live into our sitting rooms.

This conflict will be a turning point in war reportage. We are beyond the days of embedded war correspondents sending censored reports from a distant front line or from a hotel far from the bombing.

The world's media were in Ukraine as the invasion unfolded. Most ignored their government's guidance to evacuate, many were soon trapped in Kyiv and other large urban areas. The work of their camera teams has been supplemented by the thousands of soldiers and civilians now equipped with a simple cell phone and subscribing to social media accounts.

We all owe a debt of gratitude to those reporters who have stayed at their posts and brought us the news from Ukraine as it unfolds. Sarah Rainsford, Clive Myrie, Matt Fry, Lindsey Hillsum, Dan Rivers, Orla Guerin, John Irvine,

Lyse Doucet, Jeremy Bowen and James Mates are some of the names and increasingly worried faces we have seen—but they have been supported by a team of editors, camera crew, drivers, interpreters and news agency staff.

On Freeview, the Russian State broadcaster continued to promote an entirely different perspective. They believe that "the West" is seeking to control Ukraine's mineral and agricultural resources, the Ukrainian government is infiltrated by Nazis and NATO wants to use Ukraine as a base to destroy Russia. They ridicule the rest of Europe for closing down fossil fuel extraction and replacing that capacity with wind farms, solar panels and dependence on Russian gas. They believe it is their trump card. We have lots of material for prayer.

The return of **"Peaky Blinders"** (BBC1) was an anti-climax compared with the real-life drama on our news bulletins. I moved to Birmingham in 1973 and never heard a single "real Brummie" mention the Peaky Blinders until the TV series started in 2013. The only reference I was aware of them in those forty years was in a duplicated history of the Jewish community, which named a tailor who provided their distinctive caps. The truth is they were just neighbourhood thugs, the sort of people we put anti-social behaviour orders on these days. Now every "real Brummie" seems to have had a great uncle who had "connections". It is claimed the programme has "put Birmingham on the map" and there are a couple of peaky blinder themed pubs. It's just another gangster story with a couple of the leading actors trying Brummie accents. Birmingham doesn't need to be on that particular "map".

Shrewsbury is a really lovely town with some exceptional people. However, **"Death by Conspiracy"** (Radio 4) shows the town in a new light as it traces how one man, Gary Matthews, got sucked into conspiracy theories about the virus, lockdown and vaccines, and eventually succumbed to the illness. The programme describes how people who hold these conspiracy theories managed to use local social media pages to draw people into their net of intrigue and suspicion.

It all got very unpleasant when Gary's family were harassed to demand a post-mortem because the diagnosis of Covid was clearly false. The podcast is still on BBC Sounds and probably worth making time to hear, as it covers a whole range of pastoral issues.

"In Patagonia with Huw Edwards" (BBC4) we learnt how Welsh speakers created a colony in Argentina 150 years ago which would protect their language and faith. We met their descendants, many of whom still speak Welsh, enjoy tea and cakes, attend chapel, go to Welsh-speaking schools and hold Eisteddfods. The attitudes of the surrounding Spanish-speaking population have changed during those 150 years, but now the Welsh connection is cherished and celebrated. It was particularly interesting to find a Welsh speaking school where the majority of the scholars come from Spanish-speaking families. Huw Edwards picked up many of the contemporary issues which face minority communities who have migrated to the UK in recent generations.

"Fantastic Beasts: a Natural History" (BBC1) could have been an opportunity for us to understand how and why descriptions of fantastic beasts made their way into scripture, folk lore and literature. Whilst the presenter, Stephen Fry, managed to put together a competent argument that our "mythological creatures" have some basis in natural history, he wasn't able to offer much more. But in a whole lifetime of going to church, reading the Bible and various commentaries, we seem to steer well clear of the subject, so perhaps I was hoping for too much.

Time to cheer up! If you discount the blasphemous dialogue, **"Kate and Koji"** (ITV3) is good value, old-fashioned humour with lots of contemporary themes. It actually made me laugh because it's believable. Brenda Blethyn makes a credible café owner in "Seagate" and Jimmy Akingbola, brilliantly portrays her customer, an over qualified asylum seeker. It will end well.

Methodist Recorder, 11th March, 2022

I Slept on the Sofa
for Mary Whitehouse

Way back in my early 20s, I was staying at the Baptist manse in Moulsecoomb, Brighton. One day Geoff, the Minister, asked if I would mind sleeping on the sofa for a couple of nights. His house guest was to be Mrs Mary Whitehouse, at that time the much ridiculed, even hated, "Clean Up TV" campaigner, and she was to have my room. I ate with her several times and even attended one of her meetings. From what I had read in the media, I expected her to be an ignorant bigot. As we spoke, I found she certainly wasn't ignorant and, whilst opinionated, it was difficult to simply dismiss her as a bigot.

Samira Ahmed took a detailed look at Mary's diaries, other contemporary sources, and spoke to people who knew and dealt with her during those campaigning years in the second half of the 20th century. In "**Archive on 4: Disgusted, Mary Whitehouse**" (BBC Radio 4) Samira Ahmed came to a similar conclusion as I had nearly fifty years earlier: that there was more than a grain of truth in some of the matters Mary raised, but on other issues she was catastrophically wrong.

Mary launched her first campaign in the early 1960s. She presented herself as a mainstream Christian on the evangelical wing of the spectrum, a teacher and a housewife. The media loved the concept of the ordinary housewife and talked up the idea that this was a spontaneous grassroots rebellion against pornography. What Samira Ahmed didn't mention was that Mary was a long-standing member of Moral Re-Armament and had a well-funded network behind her. I challenged Mary about this in our few days together, and it was the one occasion she seemed uncomfortable.

What Mary got right, was that modern technology would offer new opportunities for the exploitation and degradation of young people, especially girls and women. She persuaded governments in the 1970s and 1980s to legislate to protect vulnerable people. Her campaigns against homosexuals lost her many potential allies, and didn't quite accord with the "hate the sin, love the sinner" formulation, then prevalent within British Christianity.

Yes, hands up, I actually liked Mary Whitehouse and certainly admired much of her work, but with many caveats. I believed she raised some important issues, not all of which have been resolved. The programme is on BBC Sounds, so if you missed it, you can make up your own mind.

Mary would have loved **"Last of the Summer Wine: 30 Years of Laughs"** (Channel 5) a wonderful retrospective on the longest-running television situation comedy. It ran for thirty-seven years and two hundred and ninety-four episodes between 1973 and 2010. At one point, it was getting twenty-two million viewers a week. Syndicated around the English-speaking world, it turned Holmfirth, in Yorkshire, where it was filmed, into a tourist attraction.

The whole programme was written by Roy Clarke, who also wrote other sitcoms including "Open All Hours" and "Keeping Up Appearances". In the 1970s, Summer Wine was seen as being revolutionary for two reasons: firstly, most of it was filmed on location; secondly, it presented a positive view of old age, at least in theory. Generally speaking, the mixture of simple storylines, strong characters and slapstick could appeal to people of all ages. There are no real villains, just a group of elderly men trying to find ways to fill their time.

But has the programme aged, as so many others have from the 1970s, with changing tastes? Perhaps the stories could have shown the old men being more helpful to their community; for example fundraising for good causes? At the time, we all shared the joke about Compo's romantic fantasy for Nora Batty and her wrinkled stockings. It reminded us that even people in their sixties could crave for sex, but did this sometimes stray into harassment? The saddest thread was the three-way conflict between Harold, his assertive wife Pearl, and his passion for Marina a lonely single woman, cast as a "mutton-dressed-as lamb" temptress. Should we still laugh?

Last week I warned "Peaky Blinders" was fiction. If you want to know more behind the myth, watch out for **"The Real Peaky Blinders"** (BBC2). Birmingham historian Carl Chinn is related to one of the families involved in the City's gang culture and tells their story.

The two-part drama documentary **"White Debt"** (Radio 4) is a challenge to white British people, as it charts a slave revolt in what is now Guyana, or Demerara as it was known in 1823. There, 70,000 enslaved people produced the sugar consumed in Europe and made massive profits for their "owners". We British still have a long way to go before we come to terms with what was done in our name all those years ago. Some of us live with the consequences, others still enjoy the legacy.

Something positive to look out for during Lent (and don't we need it?) **"Pilgrimage"** (BBC2) returns with three new sixty minute slots, following seven well-known personalities of differing faiths and beliefs as they embark on a journey together of religious and spiritual awakening across land and sea, from Ireland to Northern Ireland and Scotland.

Over fifteen days, the seven pilgrims will follow in the footsteps of the sixth-century Irish monk Saint Columba, seeking out his legacy as a key figure in early British Christianity, who helped spread the faith from Ireland to Scotland and beyond.

Methodist Recorder, 18th March, 2022

Ritualised Abuse
in plain sight on our TV screens

Take a dysfunctional relationship, put the protagonists in front of a live TV audience, make use of "lie detector tests"—which are just marginally more accurate than tossing a coin—let people who really need detailed counselling fight it out, and then cry crocodile tears when someone gets hurt.

"Death on Daytime" (Channel 4) takes a detailed look at the impact of "The Jeremy Kyle Show" on those who made and appeared on it. Several suicides later, we see how ritualised abuse of some of the most marginalised people in our country was played out in plain sight on daytime television for fourteen years.

During three thousand episodes, about twenty-thousand people put their most intimate worries in front of a million viewers. The programme purported to promote conflict resolution, but the bullying tone of the presenter, and the deliberate winding up of the participants, made for riveting TV—at least for some.

The "guests"—perhaps "victims" may be a better word— were mainly white and working-class (as were the studio audience) the only group in our society that the rest are still allowed to mock. Sometimes the programme ended in violence, in which case "security" would intervene. One studio assault ended in court and the judge referred to the show as a "human form of bear baiting".

It all came to an end when a man was berated for "failing" a lie detector test that apparently showed he had not been faithful to his lover. A few days later, he committed suicide and the show was pulled. However, this exposé reveals that there was another suicide very soon after the show was launched and many people had serious problems after appearing. I'm aware of one teenager who was mercilessly bullied after breaking down in tears on the show. There were plenty of warning signs that were ignored. But those who profit don't care what happens to working-class people after their dubious moment of fame. Speaking of which, no one mentioned any fees for the victims. It was cheap TV in more ways than one.

"Couples Therapy" (BBC2) provides a contrast to Jeremy Kyle. It gives middle-class intellectual New Yorkers the opportunity to discuss their problems with Dr Orna Guralnik.   Set in a studio designed to look like a consulting room, the atmosphere is intended to enable dialogue and exchange. Despite the sympathetic environment, it still seems strange that two people in long-standing relationships would want to share their most intimate problems with millions of others.

Sadly, dysfunctional relationships can have a devastating impact far beyond those initially involved. The **"Disappearance of Shannon Matthews"** (Channel 5) describes the chaotic circumstances of 2008, in which a mother conspired with others to fake her daughter's kidnap. Just nine months earlier, Madelaine McCann, then aged three, had disappeared in Portugal. Eye-watering rewards were offered for her safe return but sadly she remains missing. Shannon Matthews's disappearance played on all the fears of what happens when girls go missing. For twenty-four days, more than three hundred police officers and countless volunteers searched and pleaded for her return.

Thankfully Shannon was found alive at the home of a member of her extended family and it turned out there had been a plan to "find" her and claim a £50,000 reward. Two very different pictures of life emerge from the housing estate in Yorkshire where the family lived. On the one hand, there was the mother with seven children by five different men, living with a man obsessed with pornographic pictures of children, and constantly having friends in to party, even when her child was supposedly missing. This was in sharp contrast to the community spirit and engagement which enabled hundreds of local volunteers to work with the police and social services to mount a massive search for the poor girl.

Watching the two episodes on catch-up will be a big investment of time, but may help in understanding the chaos and consequences of the dysfunctional families that, hopefully, find love and welcome at our churches.

At least **"The Witchfinder"** (BBC2) is played out by actors, rather than real people, with Tim Key in the title role and Daisy May Cooper as his prize catch, Thomasine. It is well acted and has some brilliant dialogue, but the idea that the persecution of women as witches during our 17th century civil war can provide a backdrop to a "comedy" is ill conceived. It certainly didn't work for me. **"The Witches Pardon"** (Radio 4) reminds us that an estimated three thousand eight hundred and seventy people, mainly women, were tried for witchcraft in Scotland. That's a lot of suffering and nothing to laugh about.

"Lent Talks" (Radio 4) are much more positive. Six people reflect on the story of Jesus's ministry and Passion from the perspective of their own personal and professional experience. Each is posted as a podcast on BBC Sounds and provide a challenge as we prepare for Good Friday.

Can anyone ever forget the moment in the 1994 that Jean Butler and Michael Flatley burst onto our screens during the interval in the Eurovision song contest? They completely upstaged the competitors with Irish dancing like it had never been seen before. **"Steps of Freedom: the Story of Irish Dance"** (BBC4) traces Irish dancing from the church halls and competitions around the world and back to the moment three hundred million of us leapt to our feet on that evening to remember.

Methodist Recorder, 25th March, 2022.

How the Ritz and a Holiday Camp have a message for Methodists

After hearing the latest Methodist Podcast about making our churches more welcoming to various groups, I did wonder if the spate of programmes about the hospitality industry had anything to teach us.

"Happy Campers: the Caravan Park" (Channel 5) features two holiday camps in the south-west, one near Looe in Cornwall, the other at Burnham-on-Sea in Somerset. The first episode focused on the team at Tencreeks, Looe, getting ready for the critical six-week school holiday period. It takes fifty staff to ensure that hundreds of guests can "relax, chill, have a drink and a Cornish pasty".

Their aim is to provide excellent customer service from the moment of arrival. One of the campers was having difficulty securing an awning to their caravan during a rain storm. Apparently, it was the wrong sort of awning and the wrong sort of ground. The customer was getting very wet and decidedly unhappy. The receptionist tried to put it right but failed; she then called on a cheerful maintenance man who soon sorted it. One more happy family!

The people who made the camp buzz were the team of "yellow coats", who are the in-house entertainers—and we witnessed two more being recruited. They had to be able to dance, sing, jolly people along and, on occasions, dress as dolphins, pirates or sharks. The selection process was an "audition" and applicants came from all over the country. The selectors were quite honest in saying that a yellow coat had to be a bit "cheesy" but the deciding factor in one case was definitely that "she will be so loved". Staff were clearly being picked on their ability to make every customer feel they are special.

We learnt again that customer service was everything in the hospitality industry when we went to London and stepped **"Inside the Ritz Hotel"** (ITV3) a repeat from 2018. Yes, there were the lavish and luxurious soft furnishings, but time and time again we were reminded that the hotel created a sense of theatre, that the staff, whatever their role, were "putting on a show" and that "the magic" began as soon as people came through the front door. Over and over again both staff and their customers stressed that every guest should feel special.

We do need some caveats: the clientele at both the holiday camp in Cornwall and the hotel in London were mainly white and apparently fit and healthy. They also had money to spend. In August, a static caravan in Cornwall comes in between £1,000 and £1,600 for a week's stay. Afternoon tea at the Ritz starts at £67 each and the cheapest room is over £500 a night. Nevertheless, it's worth asking, how do people feel when they walk through the front doors of their local Methodist church for the first time and meet us? These programmes are worth watching.

So, it was disappointing but illuminating to hear **"An Inclusive Methodist Church"** (Methodist Podcast) in which several people expressed the belief that our churches were unwelcoming to people with certain characteristics such as race, disability, gender and sexuality. The most striking was the contribution from a young woman who used a wheelchair and found that when she moved away from her home church it was hard to find another that accepted her and her wheelchair. But I do wonder if being "inclusive" is much wider than presented here? In my circuit, we have just closed two churches and in several others congregations are admitting that they are close to calling it a day. I have a cousin who, once a year, goes for tea at the Ritz but has never set foot in her local church. I wonder how many of the Tencreek campers or staff have any experience of Christian worship? Hundreds pass our doors every day, but few come in. Perhaps we need to learn some very simple lessons in hospitality and welcome?

Incidentally, I gather several readers don't understand how to access the excellent Methodist Church podcasts. They are worth checking out on a regular basis. Just go to a search site, such as Google on your laptop or smart phone, and type "Methodist Podcasts" and up they pop.

Meanwhile, I've been having a look at the TBNUK channel. You can find it on Freeview 65. The business model means that it tends to be dominated by US based evangelists who buy space and, to be honest, sell books, but there are some UK based contributors as well. It is worth having a look because many people in our congregations watch the channel. Some of the contributions are just head and shoulders to camera, but others are more creative. I particularly liked a recent episode of **"Living Proof"** (TBNUK) featuring Beth Moore, who spoke in very earthy terms about the scandals which have perplexed many evangelical organisations in the US.

Beth has recently separated from several other evangelicals over their endorsement of Donald Trump despite his attitude to women.

Finally, I'm tempted to review myself. A couple of weeks ago I was asked onto the **"Jeremy Vine Show"** (Radio 2) to speak about accents, especially Cockney. I even mentioned the Methodist Recorder**.** It's the episode entitled "Mariupol and Fish and Chips" on BBC Sounds for the next fortnight.

Methodist Recorder, 1st April, 2022

The Trauma Faced by Victims
of war and survivors of rape

It is forty years since the war in the South Atlantic. The Argentinians invaded the Falkland Islands and landed an occupation force on South Georgia in 1982. There was a tiny British settlement and the invasion was immediately seen as a snub to the British. The victory was seen as a vindication of Mrs Thatcher and changed the political climate in her favour. But many servicemen faced years of trauma.

The **"Falklands War: the Untold Story"** (Channel 4) reminded us that the whole operation was a huge gamble that, on several occasions, came very close to disaster. Right from the start, it seemed that the command structure was dysfunctional, with political pressure to grab eye-catching headlines. The SAS effectively went rogue but were able to pick up some very useful technology from the Americans. The help of the Chilean government proved invaluable and may explain why Thatcher defended the criminal Pinochet till the bitter end. By the time it was all over, two hundred and fifty British servicemen had been killed, along with six hundred and forty-nine Argentines. War correspondent Max Hastings clearly thought the war had done the UK a great deal of good.

Meanwhile, British, French and American arms manufacturers had the opportunity to see their products used in action, much as we are seeing in Ukraine today. Wars and rumours of wars are good for business. Stuck right at the end of this fascinating programme was the reminder that the death toll is only part of the cost, as old soldiers, all too briefly, spoke of the trauma they had endured during the last forty years.

There was a more nuanced reminder of trauma in **"Beyond Reasonable Doubt: Britain's Rape Crisis"** (BBC1) as a crew went on the front line with Derbyshire Police to find out why only just one in a hundred reported rapes in England and Wales result in a conviction. Quite rightly, the programme allowed the victims themselves to speak, rather than have others speak for them. There were some harrowing testimonies of how they weren't believed, had enormous doubts themselves and sometimes came close to being suicidal. Unusually for a documentary about police and women in the current climate, the detectives came over as professional, focused, committed and able to both empathise and sympathise with the victims.

"Beyond reasonable doubt" is the phrase that judges and defence lawyers use in the last stages of a court case, and the Crown Prosecution Service is reluctant to take a case to course unless they are certain they can win. Given that much of the case is deciding whose story to believe, and often historic, allegations of rape are difficult to prove with such a high legal standing. Nevertheless, Dame Vera Baird, the Victims' Commissioner, gave some important pointers to improving the justice system to create a more realistic chance of justice being done.

This is a difficult programme to watch, and does contain some very upsetting scenes. It's on iPlayer for another eleven months and well worth watching by anyone with a professional or pastoral interest in sexual violation.

However, I would hesitate before encouraging a rape victim to watch it without appropriate support.

I rarely listen to **"Saturday Live"** (Radio 4) unless I'm driving. So, it was a surprise to catch a fascinating story a couple of weeks ago. Martyn Bradley was aged twelve when, in 1961, his great grandfather gave all his great grandchildren a pocket watch, except him, on the grounds that he was adopted. That was the first he knew that his parents had adopted him. They were active Baptists. The story they had been told was that his biological mother, who they named, had been raped aged 16 in the Congo, where her parents were serving as missionaries. She had been sent back to England where she gave birth in a Baptist maternity home. He didn't tell his adoptive parents that he wanted to find his natural mother as he began his life-long search.

Letters to the Baptist Church and later internet searches yielded little information. The searches which caused great pain were those of ship's passenger manifests from the Congo. Then one day, he tried a new app and searched all ships from Africa in 1949. Up popped his mother's name and a whole new world opened to him. His natural mother was not the daughter of a Baptist family in the Congo. Her parents were leading Methodists in South Africa, his grandfather even being the head teacher at the Healdtown Methodist School, the *alma mater* of Nelson Mandela, and other leading members of the Africa National Congress. Martyn is now in touch with his sisters, found a whole new family and published a book about his quest.

Opinions in our household are strictly divided over the sitcom **"Not Going Out"** (BBC1). I love it, my wife hates it. Now just beginning a twelfth series, it charts the relationship between a disorganised unambitious working-class man, Lee, played by Lee Mack, and his middle-class wife, Lucy, played by Sally Bretton. Part of the drama surrounded the interaction between their parents, with the late Bobby Ball playing Lee's unreconstructed father, Frank, against the urbane middle-class, Wendy and Geoffrey, played by Deborah Grant and Geoffrey Whitehead. Bobby Ball is seriously missed and Lee desperately needs his best friend, Hugh Dennis, to return as Toby. The slimmed down cast doesn't deliver this time.

Methodist Recorder, 8th April, 2022

Cadbury "Exposed" is a bit like being bitten by the Easter bunny

The impact of the Quaker Cadbury family on Birmingham has been profound. Generations wanted to work at the chocolate factory with the employee facilities and decent pay. The very fortunate ones were able to live on the spacious Bourneville village estate in sturdy houses, tree-lined roads, community halls and a ban on public houses. Charities based on the Cadbury fortune still provide essential funding for good causes across the West Midlands. We all feel reassured with the promise on every bar of Dairy Milk that "the education and training we provide makes for happier farmers and thriving local communities".

So, a television programme called **"Cadbury Exposed"** (Channel 4) felt like being bitten by the Easter bunny. Cadbury's is now owned by Mondelez, an international food company based in Chicago, with interests in over 150 countries. Reporter Antony Barnett went undercover in Ghana to find out more about the cocoa that makes the chocolate for our Easter eggs. He found young children working in extremely dangerous conditions farming the pods which provide the beans exported to the UK.

Although Cadbury's chocolate products boast a "Cocoa Life" logo, the conditions for the farmers are still very tough. It appeared to be very easy to find children out in the plantations wearing no protective clothing and wielding dangerous machetes as they cleared the land and cut open the pods. This seemed to go well beyond children helping on the farm for pocket money, with missed schooling and ever present risk.

Mondelez, of course, say they are doing everything they can to provide ethically-sourced cocoa—but this report shows they are not succeeding. Cocoa farmers are among the poorest in the world and a decent price for their produce would make an immediate difference to the lives of so many.

As we process the horrors of Ukraine, we need to remember that the memories and loss of all involved will be with us for many years. In **"The Open Box"** (Radio 4) we hear how Gail McConnell is still trying to understand her father's death after he was shot in front of her—then aged three—in 1984. She tells about her "Dad Box", the collection of papers about his life and death. There is much in there, but not Dad. Both her parents were committed Christians and we hear that his certainty of eternal life is of little help to his daughter. Although there are no obvious answers, the programme may help us understand. It is on BBC Sounds for another year.

"The Fall of the House of Maxwell" (BBC2) tells one of the most remarkable, but tragic, stories of the last seventy years. Robert Maxwell had risen from a private soldier in the Czech army in exile to become a commissioned British army officer, decorated for bravery. His entire family had been killed by the Nazis. He moved to Britain after the war, set up a very successful publishing company and within twenty years was elected as a Labour MP. In so many ways, this could have been a great success story—but even in the 1960s there were those who were keen to sneer at Maxwell, the Jewish outsider.

Maxwell's gift with languages enabled him to create contacts across Europe, but led to accusations that he was a double, or even triple, agent for protagonists in the Cold War. We were constantly reminded that his vast country home wasn't his, it was rented from Oxford corporation, so a glorified "council house".

When I met Bob Maxwell, he always seemed a little larger than life, very keen to be accepted as a committed Labour supporter. We were all delighted when he bought the **"Daily Mirror"** in the 1980s and began to counter the narrative from Murdoch's **"Sun"**. But what we didn't know was that his finances were in a mess. He wasn't the only company boss in that period to raid the pension fund to keep his businesses afloat, but he didn't pay it back before he died.

Efforts were made to scapegoat his sons Kevin and Ian, but conspiracy to defraud charges were thrown out. His daughter Ghislaine is now facing life imprisonment on sex trafficking charges. This story still has a long way to run.

It has been tempting to write a lengthy review of **"Banned! The Mary Whitehouse Story"** (BBC2) but readers will recall that I covered a Radio 4 programme about her just a few weeks ago. Last week, I caught up with Freeview channel 91 who are currently airing the 1970s **"Monty Python's Flying Circus"** (That's TV) a major peak-time comedy programme at the time. In one episode, a full third of the programme was devoted to lampooning Mary Whitehouse and her "Clean Up TV Campaign". Whatever we think of Mary, with both radio and television still carrying documentaries about her, she certainly had an impact that echoes through the decades.

When **EastEnders** (BBC1) was launched in 1985, Mary Whitehouse was one of its earliest critics. A very interesting character was launderette manager Dot Cotton, played by June Brown, who died last week aged ninety-five. Both Dot and June were Christians. I must admit, I wasn't always comfortable with Dot when she was spouting Bible verses and referring to her Christian faith. However, her portrayal of the gossipy East End matriarchs I knew as a child, was brilliant.

Methodist Recorder, 15th April, 2022

The Pain and Joy
of family connections

Over thirty years ago, I was working at the headquarters of the Methodist-led National Children's Home in London. I was called to reception to meet a jolly red faced Australian who wanted to see "the Top Man". He handed me over a holdall and said, "I want to give something back. Best thing you guys did for me was to put me on that boat to Australia. This is my first trip back and I want to say 'thank you'." And with that, he was gone. The holdall contained bundles of bank notes, several thousands in all.

So, it was with some mixed feelings that I watched **"Long Lost Family: Shipped to Australia"** (ITV1) which had been billed as revealing a "shocking and disgusting part of British history". We heard the story of some of the many children who had been taken from our children's homes and transported out to the colonies. It solved two problems. The dominions, especially Australia, wanted more white people, and the British social care system was relieved of the cost of keeping children whose parents were unable to care for them.

However, the stories of each of the children were very different. Some were told that their parents had died in the war, whilst they were actually alive and seeking to reunite their families. Siblings were broken up and letters between them held back by those responsible for their care. Some of the children suffered physical, emotional and sexual abuse. There were harrowing stories of elderly men trying to meet their long-lost brothers.

The NCH wasn't mentioned, but I was curious find out more about our denominational involvement. The Independent Inquiry into Child Sexual Abuse reported in 2018 that NCH's contribution to migration to Australia was comparatively small, that the children were accompanied by NCH Sisters and the practice was stopped by the mid-1950s, as NCH became increasingly unhappy with the care provided for the migrant children.

A more positive story of long-lost relatives was provided by **"DNA Journey"** (ITV1) which revealed the family backgrounds of the Olympic gold medal skaters Jayne Torvill and Christopher Dean. Chris found that members of his family had converted to Mormonism and migrated to Utah and that another ancestor was a leading trade unionist miner. Jayne was astonished to find that one of her relatives was a London policeman and had captained West Ham United. Jayne and Chris are such nice people, it was good to see them smile as their stories unfolded. Well researched and well told. Worth a catch-up on ITV Hub!

"Only Fools and Horses" is one of the nation's favourite sitcoms. We still laugh at the antics of three men living together in a council tower block in South London. As the series develops, the two brothers discover love interests and eventually marry Raquel and Cassandra.

"Woman's Hour" (Radio 4) recently introduced us to the actors who played Raquel (Tessa Peake-Jones) and Cassandra (Gwyneth Strong) in the comedy. They spoke about their time in the sitcom and remarked that there was never a scene where it was just the two of them, there always being at least one male character in the frame. They told of how hard they found it not to laugh during the takes in front of a live audience. But what really impressed was the friendship with the other actors and being part of a happy family—the sign of a good sitcom.

Tessa and Gwyneth are about to begin a summer tour via Derby, Malvern and Truro of a recent adaption of "Ladies of Letters", telling the story of two recently widowed women through their letters to one another. It may make a nice evening out.

It's never much fun being harangued about health and exercise as it always makes me and my mates feel failures. **"Just One Thing with Michael Mosley"** (Radio 4) seems to be aimed at those of us who are putting off making the great leap into healthier lifestyles. Over ten weeks, Mosley will be suggesting another easy step that can transform our well-being. He starts with the humble beetroot, providing reliable evidence that it is something of a wonder vegetable. It is best eaten baked or roasted or as a drink. It provides energy, keeps heart rate down and, even gentlemen, helps in other respects. Each episode lasts only fifteen minutes, so when I have a curry with the lads tonight I'm going to suggest they catch up on BBC Sounds.

We never got around to seeing the film "Bridget Jones's Diary", even though many of our women friends raved about it. The documentary **"Being Bridget Jones"** (BBC4) celebrates the 25th anniversary of its initial publication as a weekly newspaper column, penned anonymously by Helen Fielding. Eventually, it became a book, which was turned into the film. It's an inspiring example of a simple idea having unforeseen consequences and, for someone, a great opportunity. It certainly provides an encouragement to see the film.

Last week's holiday was cancelled: we had Covid. But it gave me an opportunity to watch some daytime TV. Top watch was **"Loose Women"** (ITV1) which veered from the trivial to the very serious with ease. I also caught up with **"M*A*S*H"** (Great TV) **"Perry Mason"** (CBS Drama) and **"The Brittas Empire"** (Forces TV) and some of the better **"Carry On"** films (ITV3). All on Freeview. Who needs to pay for Netflix?

Methodist Recorder, 6th May, 2022

Breast Cancer, the Menopause
and a spiky woman police officer

Television and radio offer us a safe way of stepping out of our comfort zones. Breast cancer and the menopause are on the radar of every man, but we very rarely find ourselves absorbed in the details. This week, we have two programmes that may be of immense help to women facing breast surgery or the menopause, but I can't help feeling that many men should make themselves sit down and watch them on catch-up or when they are repeated.

However, my entertainment pick must be the brilliant new **"D.I.Ray"** (ITV). This is more than just another police drama. Parminder Nagra, who we would have first spotted proving that women can play football in the film, "Bend it Like Beckham", dons a police uniform to play a very spiky Detective Inspector. She isn't in uniform for the opening sequence, she's in mufti buying a bottle of wine and another customer assumes that she is a member of the shop's staff. Within minutes, she is caught up with a disturbed man wielding a knife and then resolves the crisis without having to resort to the overwhelming armed and lethal force which was quickly assembled.

We see her encounter the casual racism that so many of us deploy without thinking. "Where are you from?" asks one of her new colleagues. "Leicester," she replies. That wasn't what he meant, so his follow up question was, "What is your heritage?" Just think about it: why is it that so many of us feel able to ask someone from an Asian background whether they are Muslim, Sikh, Christian or Hindu? This programme, and I certainly hope there is a follow up series, may have a lot to teach us. And it's an edge-of-the-seat story.

"Julia Bradbury: Breast Cancer and Me" (ITV1) is a world away from the healthy outdoor walks we normally associate with Julia. We follow her through the pain, exasperation, anger and, hopefully, full recovery, after finding a lump in her left breast and a biopsy, which revealed she needed a mastectomy. Just a few days before the operation, we see her lauded on the red carpet at an awards ceremony, quickly followed by an upsetting piece to camera in the middle of the night as she shares her fears and tears about what is to happen.

The camera doesn't hold back and we see some graphic images of her chest marked up ready for the op, together with an intimate injection in preparation. Fortunately, we do not see the actual operation. The post-op shots of her breasts showcase the wonders of modern surgery and reconstruction.

Julia's life went on hold once she had been told, but she was still a wife, mother and daughter. She describes the dilemmas about what to say and to whom, and her worries about aftercare, both physical and psychological. Like many other couples, my wife and I have gone from fear to clear, but if she had been diagnosed, this programme would have been a very helpful preparation.

"Davina McCall: Sex, Mind and the Menopause" (Channel 4) is a rallying call for a better understanding and better treatment for women as they go through the menopause. There are some stunning statistics of how many women lose their jobs or reduce their hours because employers are unable to recognise the impact on women's physical and mental health. The menopause even has an "evil little sister", the peri-menopause, whose onset is well before periods stop buts includes familiar symptoms such as brain fog, sleeplessness and a loss of interest in sexual intimacy.

Sadly, many women are expected to suffer in silence and the postcode lottery for hormone replacement therapy on the NHS indicates this. Research in the US suggests that early HRT and testosterone treatment can reduce the impact, enabling women to focus more clearly during the more difficult times. Early treatment can also reduce the risk of other conditions such as breast cancer and Alzheimers.

"By the Grace of God" (BBC4) the acclaimed drama based the true story of three men who were abused as children by a priest, will be on iPlayer for the next three months. It is in French with subtitles and runs for two hours, and may be helpful to those involved with safeguarding issues.

"What Really Happened in the 90s" (Radio 4) gives us an opportunity to look back on the day before yesterday. Do you remember "cool Britannia", "girl power" and the fall of communism? For many, it was a period of so much optimism but even the seeds of the poisonous war in Ukraine were sown in that decade. But if you really want strife on your wireless, drop into **"The Archers"** (Radio 4) .

The new broom at Grey Gables is certainly sweeping out the cobwebs, and most of the staff.

Fellow Hackney lad's **"Jay Blades: No Place Like Home"** (Channel 5) takes a nostalgic walk around our childhood home. In places, he is a bit too rosy-eyed. It wasn't always easy living on a Hackney council estate in the 1960s, and I don't buy "the Krays were good to their mother" stuff, but it was fascinating to see how a Black man interpreted our shared childhood environment, especially his realisation that some in Hackney benefited from slavery. Rather tellingly, Jay remarks that this isn't like the history he was taught at school, but much more interesting.

Methodist Recorder, 13th May, 2022

There Is More to Buying an Electric Car
than a green preen

Ok, I'll admit it: I'm not interested in cars. Motoring programmes such as "Top Gear" are boring. But this week, tucked away in the schedules, was a programme which I really do commend to anyone who is thinking about buying or replacing a car in the near future. I also look at another Methodist podcast channel, and make a bold prediction about the sitcom of the 2020s. But first, cars.

In **"Should I Buy an Electric Car?"** (Channel 5) journalist Alex Conran asked the questions that anyone thinking of making the switch from petrol or diesel should be asking. Just minutes into the narrative, we are reminded that buying an electric car is much more serious than just a green preen to bolster our carbon-suppressing credentials. On average, a new electric car will cost double that of a new petrol-powered car, although that is expected to drop as production gears up to meet the demand. But there is some good news: servicing costs are lower.

The real problems are that the infrastructure to charge the cars is still in the early stages. If you have a drive outside your house it is easy enough to run a cable from the domestic electricity supply. Things get more complicated once the car is parked on the street. Cables between the house and the car will inevitably cross public footpaths and could prove to be a trip hazard with the liability falling on the owner, should anyone be injured. Knowing the parking rows that erupt in the Victorian streets around our inner-city church with several car owners in every house, it's obvious there are going to be some violent confrontations.

Paying for power from a public charger can be a nightmare. There aren't enough and paying has to be through websites, each with their own registration and payment procedures. Unlike filling up with petrol, it takes longer for a car to charge. But Alex Conran borrowed an electric car to film and fell in love with it, as does everyone else who takes the plunge. You can find the programme on My5 for the next twelve months.

You won't find many electric cars in the fifth series of **"Bangers and Cash"** (Yesterday) which takes a nice relaxing view of the vintage car trade. The story focusses on the entrepreneurial auction family the Mathewsons, led by grandad Derek, his sons and grandsons. Each programme tells the story of old cars, usually from the 1960s, 1970s and 1980s, which are put up for auction often by elderly people, usually closing down their lives. During the collection, valuation and sale, we hear a lot about the lost world of the British car industry and our social history. And you will love the banter as the family cope with the pressures of auctioning four thousand cars and piles of memorabilia each year from their headquarters at Thornton-le-Dale in North Yorkshire. You don't have to know anything about cars to enjoy this programme.

Meanwhile, Britain's three thousand two hundred miles of motorway are already carrying ten times the traffic for which they were built. A new series of **"The Motorway"** (Channel 5) goes behind the scenes as the traffic officers from the Highway Agency manage our motorways and A roads. Somewhere in each region there is a massive control room with CCTV showing all the major junctions and sorting out traffic flows. We followed the work of the traffic officers who respond to incidents, some of which seem bizarre. Personally, I found it very reassuring that there is someone responsible to keep us moving.

There's another Methodist podcast channel! **"One Voice"** (https://methodist-churches-northampton.org.uk/podcasts) is produced by John Rose, an experienced professional radio presenter with several top-rated commercial stations. The Northampton District have got a real gem here, so I hope they don't mind me saying that it should be a national, even international, resource. The twenty-three episodes include local items such as the Kingsthorpe Girls' Brigade—which will be really interesting to anyone in youth work anywhere—but also undocumented migrants and the Dalit community's contribution to Christianity. I will admit that the May episode includes an interview about how I write this review for the **Methodist Recorder**, but I won't be offended if you skip over to the inspiring story of a Brazilian presbyter who has been stationed in Stoke Newington, London.

Until recently, religious news broadcasting has been limited to just a few spots on Radio 4, this podcast and the "Connexional" podcast show that new channels are available. Just Google "Northampton Methodist Podcasts" and several links will appear.

Time to make a prediction: In the 2050s those of us who are left will be enjoying watching **"Here We Go"** (BBC1) to remind ourselves of family life in the roaring 20s. The story is told through the camera of a teenage son who is filming a real-time documentary about his family for a media studies course. Paul Howick plays Dad, Paul Jessop, who was, at one time, a promising archer and now desperate for attention, self-esteem and money, much like many other dads. Katherine Parkinson, formerly a receptionist in "Doc Martin" plays Rachel, his wife, who works hard to keep things together for her ungrateful children and detached husband. Dad's mum, played by Alison Steadman, best known as Gavin's mum in "Gavin and Stacey", keeps popping by with her latest "helpful" idea. You will laugh. Promise! Ideal Friday night viewing.

Methodist Recorder, 20th May, 2022

Let's Have Some Luvly Jubbly
for the Jubilee knees up!

Let's face it, after the last two years, we are all ready for a bit of a knees-up, and the Jubilee holidays may give us the break we need. And what better way to enjoy ourselves, than with a good feed?

"The Jubilee Pudding: 70 Years in the Baking" (BBC1) showed off some of our nation's creativity in the kitchen. Over two thousand people had submitted recipes for a pudding fit for the Queen. The recipes were finally whittled down to fifty and then again to find the five finalists. It was a competition, but much more relaxed than the bake-off genre with macho time limits and critical eyes and taste buds.

Unsurprisingly, the final contestants were women (more about that later) and several of them mentioned their grandmothers as major influences on their cooking. The theory was that the chosen pudding should be easy to make with ready-to-hand ingredients. That's not how it looked from where I sat! All the contestants had great ideas about what their pudding would represent. I certainly warmed to Susan from Scotland, who wanted to represent our four nations, and Shabnam, who grew up in Mumbai and hoped to tickle our more diverse palettes.

Jemma's Lemon Swiss roll and amaretti trifle was chosen by the panel of experts, led by Mary Berry. To be honest, it did look rather complicated to make but I enjoyed the bright orange that reminded me of the Jubbly we drank from its tetrahedron cardboard pack, way back to celebrate the Coronation.

If women create our Jubilee pudding, we should be honest and recognise that holidays do create extra work in the kitchen. As I tell Mrs H, these are not occasions to prove that she is a domestic goddess so, like lots of husbands, I offer to share the load by suggesting we eat out, or get a takeaway.

One place we won't book for our Jubilee treat will be the JCR Global Buffet in Watford. **"All-You-Can-Eat Buffets: How Do They Really Do It?"** (Channel 5) went behind the scenes of one of the biggest restaurants in the UK, which serves 350 dishes from eight global cuisines, to three thousands guests a day. It is an amazing operation with constant deliveries, creative chefs, a very committed waiting staff and a firm, but flexible, front-of-house team. If you have a big family or a large congregation (one church booked for three hundred) it will probably be cost effective. Be warned though, the moment you take your seat you are being timed without much scope for a leisurely digestif or coffee.

If you decide to go for a Jubilee takeaway, someone else can bring it to your door. **"Deliveroo: How Do They Really Do It?"** (Channel 5) was made without the co-operation of the company, whose participation was via terse and defensive written statements. We already spend a staggering £3 billion per year on these services, fuelled by young people who seem to have more money than sense. Deliveroo charge the customer for delivery and the use of their app. They then take a commission from the supplier. On average, you will pay 30-40 per cent more than if you pick it up yourself. That all adds up if you are feeding family and friends. Delivery is by self-employed riders, who compete to make as many drops as possible. Different foods lose their heat at different rates. Burgers, "fries" (sort of skinny chips) and pizzas cool faster than cheesy chips, fried chicken or curry. When you place an order, give an accurate address and any useful detail, such as "opposite City Road Methodist Church". Give them a wave when you know they are near. If you become dependent on Deliveroo, Uber or Just Eat, play them off against one another so the algorithms offer you special deals. Incidentally, if you need a pint of milk, it will cost £5.58.

Next week will certainly be a TV bonanza with Jubilee-themed programmes. Highlights will include a look at the Queen's private family photos and films, another Jubilee baking programme, a special edition of Grayson Perry's art slot, a service of thanksgiving, a parade and a party at the palace. Let's hope they are an improvement on **"The Queen's Platinum Jubilee Celebration"** (ITV1). The acts and displays were wonderful but poor lighting, inept commentary, too few cameras, and advertising breaks detracted from what could have been some special and memorable TV moments. Phillip Schofield and Julie Etchingham, the presenters, overdid the participation of the actor Tom Cruise, who seemed to be on show to promote his latest film. It would have been better on the BBC.

Away from the Jubilee, radio comes into its own with **"Drama: The Reckoning"** (Radio 4) a three-part series based on Charles Nicholl's true crime mystery on the death of the play-write Christopher Marlow. The crime may have been committed in 1593 but in three gripping episodes we find it is far from a 'cold case'. It is still on BBC Sounds.

If you were transfixed with "Normal People" a couple of years ago, you may like to catch up with the twelve-part **"Conversations with Friends"** (BBC3) which is made by the same team. An unhurried drama, which builds slowly, you very quickly work out that someone is going to get badly hurt. You can watch it week by week or binge watch the whole series on iPlayer.

Methodist Recorder, 27th May, 2022

Hunting Witches, Abusing MPs,
and even Private Godfrey faces abuse

In 1991, a Methodist Minister accused me of being a witch. He was quite serious. He was accompanied by another member of his church and told several of my close friends. His "evidence" was sightings of some books on the occult I has used for some research, which were seen by a fellow Christian who had come to our home to do some odd jobs. It was an abusive encounter, but I was able to walk away.

Just four hundred years before, in 1591, the midwife Agnes Sampson was unable to walk away from similar allegations. After interrogation, torture and a forced, false confession, she was garrotted and then burnt in Edinburgh for being a witch. In four brilliantly presented episodes, **"The Witch Hunt: Lucy Worsley Investigates"** (BBC2) shows how Christian people created an atmosphere of repression and fear which suited those with power, ambition, and a desire to keep women firmly in their place.

Agnes Sampson was the first of an estimated two thousand five hundred people, most of them women, who were killed during the witch-hunting mania which gripped Scotland in the following seventy or eighty years. Those accused would be stripped naked, have every hair on their body shaved and then pierced by two-inch nails as the men searched for the "Devil's mark". No part of the body was spared, including nipples and genitalia. Victims were broken spiritually and mentally, agreeing to 'confessions' which sealed their fate and implicated others.

At a time when, for example, there is a growing tide of anti-Semitism and Islamophobia, it is worth Christians, including Methodists, simply pausing and asking how we think, talk and act towards others. The series is on iPlayer; it's not entertainment, but important to watch.

A few years back, I took over running the office of a senior woman politician and had to deal with a backlog of emails. Most were invites, constituency problems plus a handful of marriage proposals! But even as a hardened political hack of the old school, I was shocked at several very abusive, sometimes highly sexual, racist messages, one or two of which referred to the politician as a "witch". Kim Leadbeater, the sister of the murdered MP Jo Cox, investigated the risks MPs and their staff face in "**MPs under Threat**" (Channel 4) and it does not make easy viewing.

Two MPs have been murdered in recent years and several others attacked. Whilst I suffered abuse as an MEP, including a suspected bomb delivered to our house, it was nothing like our MPs, especially women, face today. Emails and social media have made the pressures more intense, but there is certainly an atmosphere which generates violent language and violent behaviour. This programme reminds us that we should pray for the safety of all who stand for election and seek to serve their communities.

There was one real treat last week with the return of **"Dad's Army"** (BBC2) the wartime sitcom about the Home Guard. The episode "Branded" tells the story of Private Godfrey's decision to leave the platoon, revealing that he was a conscientious objector to military service in the previous war. Probably gay, and a Quaker, we see the vileness which otherwise decent people can express to a vulnerable man when challenged. It is funny, but will make you weep. Certainly, the most moving episode. It's on iPlayer for another fortnight.

The Michaela Community School in Wembley is headed by Katherine Birbalsingh, who has been dubbed **"Britain's Strictest Headmistress"** (ITV1). Even watching the school through the lens of a TV camera felt uncomfortable. Some of the interactions between teachers, which verged on bullying of children half their size, should not have been shown—at least with the children identifiable. All sorts of claims were made about the school's success in creating a learning environment, and both teachers and schoolchildren in my family have expressed concern about the lack of discipline in their schools. But humiliation is surely unacceptable? One thing I did notice is that those few parents we met were both present and apparently first generation migrants. I'm not certain Ms Birbalsingh's approach could easily be replicated in the white working-class schools here in the Black Country.

The BBC sometimes makes an easy target, but in the discussions about future funding let us hope the wonderful local radio network is both protected and celebrated. The presenter of our local station's morning programme was recently featured as the face behind the voice in the "Radio Times". **Kathryn Stanczyszyn** (BBC WM) known with affection as "Stanners", tells of her career, which has involved speaking to survivors of the Grenfell fire, meeting MP colleagues of Jo Cox, hours after her murder, and exposing out-of-date personal protection equipment which was sent to Birmingham hospitals at the start of the pandemic. Send your local BBC radio station news from your church and community. They will be missed if we lose them.

Those who enjoy **"Secrets of the London Underground"** (Yesterday) can look forward to a special edition in June. Tim and Siddy will be exploring the Kingsway tram tunnel, closed since 1953.

Methodist Recorder, 3rd June, 2022

THE YEAR THE QUEEN DIED

The Hope and Optimism
Of the Coronation
and Coventry Cathedral

The TV schedules and news channels have certainly been full of news and nostalgia related to the Jubilee. During this century, we have had one every ten years, but for many, the Silver Jubilee in 1977 is a distant memory. For a diminishing number of us, the Coronation in 1953 is still the premier royal event of our lifetime, so I suspect that I wasn't the only "senior citizen" to watch **"Secrets of the Queen's Coronation"** (Channel 4) . No one under seventy will have the faintest first-hand memory of those amazing few weeks of anticipation, colour and celebration.

In 1953, the country was recovering from war. Our home was an asbestos framed "pre-fab", hurriedly built on the site of a V-Bomb attack. My Dad had managed to get a pre-war TV and we all tuned in to watch the Coronation service. When I say "we all", I mean most of our relatives, friends and a lot of neighbours. Lots of beer was drunk, salmon sandwiches eaten and jelly scoffed as we peered at a twelve-inch black and white screen.

Sixty-nine years later, we are able to see the meticulous preparations that went into staging those few precious hours of communications history. The ladies-in-waiting and a page boy told us their story, but it would have been interesting to hear more from the thousands of servicemen who lined the route and marched through the drizzle. The programme did convey the feeling of optimism that many of us can remember from our childhood; sadly, that may not be the case for the children who witness the next Coronation.

An expression of the optimism of post-war Britain was the determination to replace the bombed Coventry Cathedral. The new building was consecrated in the summer of 1962. **"Coventry Cathedral: Building for a New Britain"** (BBC4) tells the amazing story of the planning and execution of the project. Sir Basil Spence, the architect, understood that it had to be more than a memorial to its predecessor. The new Cathedral would be about forgiveness, reconciliation and hope, taking the visitor and worshipper on their emotional, spiritual and personal journey of faith. Whether it's your first or a return visit, this programme is well worth watching on iPlayer before you set out.

Benjamin Britten's War Requiem was one of the first public events to be held at Coventry Cathedral. It's normally presented as a choral work but to mark the centenary of the start of the First World War, the English National Opera decided to perform it as a piece of theatre at the London Coliseum. **"Britten's War Requiem: Staging a Masterpiece"** (BBC4) follows the story from the initial rough plans to the final rehearsals. Britten brought together the Latin Mass with the poetry of Wilfred Owen, who was killed in the final weeks of that terrible war. Britten wanted to create a sense of urgency, with passion and a commitment that such a war would never happen again. It was humbling to watch the soloists and one hundred and twenty-strong chorus rehearsing and mentally preparing for the performance, especially the forty children. Hopefully, the War Requiem will be staged again.

A weekly review of **"Great British Railway Journeys"** (BBC4) is tempting but probably would not be welcomed by every reader. Michael Portillo has managed the move from Tory Cabinet minister to much-loved television presenter specialising in trains. From contacts in the heritage railway community, I'm told he certainly appears to knows his stuff. In one recent episode, he visited the editorial offices of "The Morning Star", the newspaper of the British Communist Party. He recalled that until the mid-60s it was known more simply as "The Daily Worker". It was only a few minutes, but must be one of the few times that the "Morning Star" has been featured in a mainstream TV programme.

Whilst we celebrate the past, it can sometimes be bit of a shock to remember what made us laugh then. Some comedy endures, such as "Dad's Army", but other "jokes" become very dated. The current series of situation comedy retrospectives has brought us **"Are You Being Served?: Secrets and Scandals"** (Channel 5). It was set in a department store, which even in the 1970s had out-dated counters, stock and attitudes. John Inman played a gay shop assistant and created the catchphrase "I'm free", which made us laugh because it was taken as an invitation for sexual activity. Mollie Sugden played a widow who lived alone with her cat, which was turned into yet more sexual innuendo. One of the critics described these jokes as "self-cleansing" because only those with a certain mindset would find them funny. To be honest, some of the scenes, especially those with old men and young women, were distinctly "pervy". It wouldn't be made today.

Meanwhile, tucked away in the schedules on a Sunday lunchtime when we're coming back from church, is the wonderful **"The Listening Project"** (Radio 4). It's a partnership between BBC Radio 4, BBC local stations and the British Library. They are gathering an archive about the way we live our lives. I'm not certain what future generations will make of the man who attaches a magnet to a piece of string and then "fishes" for metal objects in rivers and ponds, but other snippets such as ambulance waiting times reflect modern Britain. Well worth a listen, either when scheduled or on BBC Sounds.

Methodist Recorder, 10th June, 2022

OMG!
Love Island returns
– but who benefits?

"Love Island" (ITV2) has started another annual eight-week run with more references to God in the first episode than can be heard in a whole year on "Songs of Praises".

We may not like it nor even see it, but the young parents in the church playgroup and the big siblings of the Boys' Brigade battalion will be transfixed, as will their Instagram feed, TikTok accounts, Twitter account and the tabloid media. So, perhaps the rest of us should understand this genre known as "reality TV".

The format of this show is to bring five men and five women in their late teens and twenties together in a villa in Spain. Their conversations are recorded, edited, and broadcast each evening. They are "coupled" by a vote from the public and expected, on their first night, to share a bed with someone they have only just met; they have no choice. During the eight weeks, they will swap partners, be dropped from the series or be augmented by the arrival of a "bombshell"—someone more physically attractive than those already there.

Most of the discussion and "games" are of a sexual nature. The women are concerned about love and personality, whereas the men are focused on physical attributes. Alongside the show is a lively discussion on social media with, for example, seven or eight thousand posts an hour on Twitter. Many posts are really vicious with offensive comments about the islanders' physical appearance, motivation and conversation. So far, three contestants have committed suicide since 2015 after appearing on the show.

Why on earth would anyone put themselves through the very public humiliation of reality TV? "**Unreal: A Critical History of Reality TV**" (Radio 4) provides some answers, many of which are sinister and disturbing. Over eight episodes, Pandora Sykes and Sirin Kale explain the emotions, formatting and economics of reality TV programmes such as "Big Brother", "Keeping Up With the Kardashians", "Made in Chelsea", "The Only Way Is Essex" and **"Love Island"**.

British reality TV started in 2000 with the launch of "Big Brother", when a group of housemates were placed in total isolation and their every move filmed. The media lapped up the nuances, confrontations, supposedly private confessions to the camera, and eventual evictions based on nominations by their peers until a winner emerged. The format was especially popular among younger people, who are difficult for advertisers to reach, and so made the commercial TV channels a lot of money.

However, a successful run on a reality show could be life-changing for the young people taking part. Jade Goody, a dental nurse from a troubled family in London's Bermondsey, is reputed to have earned £8 million between her appearance in "Big Brother" in 2002 and her death from cervical cancer in 2009. Goody could not sing, dance, nor act, but managed to become a "celebrity" presenting her own shows, endorsing products, and making personal appearances.

Contestants for **"Love Island"** claim they are there to seek love and a special relationship. But most are signed-up with an agent who promotes their brand on social media and opens up lucrative sponsorship deals as "influencers". One contestant, evicted after just a few days, saw her social media following jump from a few hundred to two million whilst on the show. That can be turned into hard cash.

Much of that cash comes from "fast fashion", in which clothing produced by exploited workers is sold cheaply and discarded after being worn just two or three times. The unwanted clothes are swamping charity shops or end up in landfill in Africa. Sykes and Kale's series is still on BBC Sounds and well worth a catch up, with an entire episode looking at **"Love Island"**.

Two new comedies on the same channel on the same night looked a good deal. **"Everything I Know About Love"** (BBC1) is set in a London flat share where four twenty-something women navigate work, finance and relationships. Based on the book by Dolly Alderton, we see the stirrings of love, rejection, blind dating, desperate texting and young women hoping to meet the man of their dreams. Some of the story lines are uncomfortable, such as a night out which includes numerous shots which remind us how vulnerable young people are in modern society. This is a romantic comedy, which we hope will have a happy ending. But **"PRU"** (BBC1) also billed as a comedy, is no laughing matter. A pupil referral unit is where very dedicated teachers try to work with children who have been excluded from mainstream schooling. It just isn't funny.

Many of our churches built in the Medieval period carry the scars of the destruction wrought by our Protestant forebears during the Reformation. If we think such vandalism belongs to the past, **"Book of the Week: Iconoclasm"** (Radio 4) brought us David Freedberg's timely work on iconoclasm both in the past and in the present. Quite rightly, we wince at the destruction by Islamic State in Iraq and Syria, but how do we feel about the campaigns to remove the statues of Confederate generals, which are a feature of many US public spaces? Freedberg's work just predates the toppling of Edward Colston's statue in Bristol, but many of us, whilst deploring the method, welcome the removal. Does that make us iconoclasts alongside Islamic State? You can find all five episodes on BBC Sounds.

Methodist Recorder, 17th June, 2022

Cor! Wotta Scorcher!
Hot summers and the Methodist who started the Glastonbury Festival

The summer of 2022 got off to a disappointing start—despite the very hot weather in France, Spain and Italy, which was all very similar to 1976. **"Heatwave: Summer of '76"** (Channel 5) reminded us just how a slight change in the isobars can bring very hot weather north. On 23 June 1976, we experienced an unusually hot day and were determined to enjoy it. We didn't know that the heatwave, without a spot of rain, would last another forty-five days.

For many, it was a brilliant summer and a welcome distraction from the industrial strife, inflation and terrorist war which was besetting these islands. However, the heat and lack of water were a foretaste of what the doomsters of climate change now predict. In many parts of the country water supplies simply ran out. We were exhorted to save water by not flushing our toilets so often, sharing a bath with a friend and forbidden from watering our gardens. Food supplies were hit by a poor harvest and domestic animals lost weight because their pasture had dried up. The most sinister and uncomfortable development was a "biblical" plague of ladybirds unleashed from their normal habitat and swarming everywhere.

The government's response was to appoint a Minister for Drought, Denis Howell, a Birmingham MP. Three days later, it started raining and I remember us pouring out of a Labour Party event and getting thoroughly wet!

There was just one little point which was hinted at by former Labour Leader, Neil Kinnock: we didn't shower and bath as often in the 1970s. Water companies claim they are now better prepared, but I'm sure we wash ourselves and our clothes more often than we did then and, so, use much more water.

Since 1970, most summers bring us the "Glastonbury Festival". After two years of Covid cancellation, it was back this year with 80-year-old Paul McCartney scheduled as the headline act. **"Glastonbury: 50 years and Counting"** (BBC2) told the story of how Methodist farmer Michael Eaves turned Worthy Farm, in Somerset, into one of the hottest showbiz venues. Eaves admitted that things happened at the festival that "some of my chapel friends would call sinful". Overall, Glastonbury is an impressive story of how a young farmer in his late twenties started a simple music festival that just grew bigger. Some of the festivals attracted up to three hundred thousand people and nightly television feeds.

Much of the money generated by TV rights and admission tickets is ploughed back into a range of charities such as Water Aid and Oxfam. In the early 80s, Eaves donated £20,000 to the Campaign for Nuclear Disarmament. He also demonstrated a spirit of hospitality when, in 1985, after a particularly nasty attack near Stonehenge on a convoy of nomadic "New Agers", Eaves invited them to stay on his farm. For several years after that there was an area for travellers next to the festival site, but this became a magnet for drug trafficking, leading to further violence. There was much talk of "ley lines" and other occult nonsense, giving the festival a special feel. But it does seem that a lot of people have a great time, make new friends and, when it rains, get very wet and muddy.

One of the headline acts at the Glastonbury Festival was David Bowie. He struggled in the early 1970s and looked set to be a one-hit wonder following an early success. Then he created the bisexual 'glam rock'. **"Archive on 4: Ziggy Stardust at 50"** (Radio 4) tells the story of his reinvention. This is well worth a listen on BBC Sounds, whatever your musical tastes.

If muddy fields in Somerset are not your choice for a holiday, you may be interested in the new series of **"Bargain Loving Brits by the Sea"** (Channel 5) . This is exactly what a British family holiday should be: no intellectual challenge, lots of pop with fish and chips, dad spending more time at the cashpoint than he had planned and, above all, buckets and spades interspersed by rain and amusement arcades. If you have happy memories of places, such as Skegness and Blackpool, this is a wonderful way to spend an hour on a Sunday evening or on My5 catch-up.

It's not anything like my week one October on the Liverpool-Leeds canal but **"The Cruise"** (Channel 5) offers a glimpse of an alternative holiday on water. No children are allowed on the "Scarlet Lady" as she sails from Miami with three thousand adult guests, known as "sailors", and a thousand-strong crew. The ship is seventeen stories high, has eight hundred cabins, twenty restaurants, and cost £650 million to build. Guests are greeted by Ryan from the "happenings cast" and assured that they are welcome. No mention is made of the economic benefits or environmental costs to the impoverished Caribbean islands the "sailors" sail pass in luxury.

Summer heat brings a craving for ice cream and lollies. A new series of **"Inside the Superbrands"** (Channel 4) returned with a visit to the Wall's factory and showed us how their products are made and marketed. Ice cream used to be a summer treat but careful marketing and more home refrigeration make it an easy-to-serve dessert for many families, all year-round. Mind you, I've never tasted anything as good as the dollop of ice cream dropped into a glass of cream soda that we had after Sunday School each week!

Methodist Recorder, 1st July, 2022

Guinness Takes the Spirit Out, but the Baptists keep it in

To those of us who love television programmes about marketing, **"Inside the Superbrands: Guinness"** (Channel 4) was a wonderful immersion into how brands must present themselves to a new generation. The director of marketing for Guinness explained that once young people strongly associate a brand with their parents or grandparents, they regard it as old fashioned and not for them. Interestingly, the latest incarnation of Guinness for a new generation will be a non-alcoholic version which tastes the same, but without the spirit.

How we as churches present ourselves to a new secularised generation was very much the theme of both our own Methodist Conference in Telford and an episode of **"Songs of Praise"** (BBC1) from the Baptist Assembly in Bournemouth.

Like Methodists, the Baptists have faced the attrition of our secular age and presenter Claire McCollum estimated that their numbers in this country had fallen to just one hundred thousand. Sadly, the hymns were not from the Assembly but they were interspersed by four very strong interviews from active Baptists. Three of those stories could probably be replicated among members of our own "Connexion": the couple who provided a home for a Ukrainian refugee family, a stroke victim who found that the illness profoundly changed her relationship with God and now supports others who have suffered a stroke, and a project to create sacred art.

The fourth interview was with Lynn Green, the General Secretary of the Baptist Assembly, who was full of enthusiasm and clarity. In just a few sentences, she explained the symbolism of new believers' baptism with total immersion represents death with Christ and the free gift of new life with Jesus. It was an idea that had grasped my penitent teenage heart shortly after my conversion.

The following day, I attended a two-hour presentation on evangelism at Methodist Conference. Had I been a teenager, I think I would have got lost after the ninety-seventh reference to "justice" and "love", which seemed to be a condition of God's love, rather than an outpouring of His divine grace. Perhaps, a future Conference should invite Lynn Green as a speaker? This episode of **"Songs of Praise"** showed that the focus on a personal faith does not exclude social action. The Baptists, as represented on this programme, have rebranded for a new generation, but unlike Guinness, have kept the spirit in!

Sixteen BBC local radio stations carried interviews with delegates to the our Annual Conference. **"Angela Kalwaites"** (BBC Radio Devon) spoke with the new President of Conference, Graham Thompson. He was able to pose the question: "Who is our neighbour?" and immediately outlined what that meant in a post-Covid Britain, with our cost of living crisis, growing mental health problems and longer NHS waiting list. The interview is still on BBC Sounds for another fortnight. It can be found one hour and seventeen minutes into the programme dated 26 July.

Barry Morley and his son James are both ordained Methodist ministers. Dad Morley received the call after a career in the coal industry. James explains how uncool it was to be a "vicar's son" rather than have a dad down the pits. James now has a very different ministry to heavy metal fans who are into Goth culture, probably as far as the music scene gets from Christianity. Their story, together with features about online safety, housing repairs, gardening and much more, are available on the **"Roots and Roofs Podcast"** of the Methodist Ministers Housing Society. This will obviously be of interest to retired Ministers and their spouses, but deserves a wider audience and will be especially useful for those with failing eyesight.

"Desert Islands Discs" (Radio 4) has been with us forever. Sometimes it feels like a celebrity publicity puff, but other episodes bring through a really human story. I remember seeing Rita Tushingham in the 1961 film "A Taste of Honey" but knew very little about the nineteen-year-old actor who shocked many with the first interracial on-screen kiss. She had answered a newspaper advert for an "ugly" woman actor. It must have been a brave step to have sought such an accolade. Throughout the audition and filming she had the support of her mother and ended winning several awards for the film.

Rita's choice of records was probably typical of a Liverpool woman whose teenage years were spent in Liverpool. She spoke about her faith, which was very much her own, incorporating bits and pieces that she had collected over the years. It did feel that she saw some of her chosen discs, especially "Bridge Over Troubled

Waters"and "You'll Never Walk Alone" as secular hymns. It is still on BBC Sounds.

Nick Robinson, for many years the BBC's political correspondent, has disappeared from our screens but has now popped up with his own radio show "**Political Thinking with Nick Robinson**" (Radio 4). One recent edition featured a conversation with the money saving expert Martin Lewis, who some see as one of the most influential journalists in the country. There was one moment that felt uncomfortable: Lewis is Jewish. This leads to him being subject to a barrage of tropes on social media about his attitude to money and a more general anti-Semitism. Despite the events of the last century, it is sad that Jews are still picked out by this wickedness. For two thousand years, Christians have hated Jews. It is time we set an example.

Methodist Recorder, 8th July, 2022

When Jagger Was Banned

The first time I realised that post-conversion Christianity may not always be harmonious was when our Minister insisted the youth club banned the Rolling Stones' latest hit "Let's Spend the Night Together". It had a fantastic beat, was great to dance to, but had some very iffy words. We tried to persuade him that Mick Jagger may have been singing to his wife, but the Minister wasn't a fool. It was banned.

Celebrating sixty years since the Stones first arrived on the pop scene, the four-part series **"My Life as a Rolling Stone"** (BBC2) features Mick Jagger, the late Charlie Watts, Keith Richards and Ronnie Wood. Each tell their story as a Stone with, as always, Mick Jagger first.

Jagger's intention as a schoolboy was to go to university and follow a conventional career. After two years at university, the lure of the pop world proved too much and he dropped out to become a musician. When the Stones first formed, they did cover songs but their manager encouraged them to write their own. He also suggested that as a counterpoint to the clean-living Beatles, they should create an anarchic and rebellious persona. We loved it! "Satisfaction" remains the all-time favourite record of many an ageing rocker, to us they easily surpassed the Beatles.

If you want to spend the night together, all these programmes are on iPlayer together with, **"The Rolling Stones Live at the Fonda"** (BBC2) where they play the entire "Sticky Fingers" album in concert for the first time and **"The Rolling Stones: Totally Stripped"** (BBC2) which follows their making of the album.

When we danced in our teens to "Let's Spend the Night Together" our assumption was that it was about two people of the opposite sex. It never occurred to many of us at the time that men could long to sleep with, still less love, another man, or a woman another woman. We knew that some people were attracted to their own sex, but they were referred to by various insulting put-downs. Not very nice at all and, to be honest, we didn't know any better.

"Freedom: 50 Years of Pride" (Channel 4) took us back to those first tentative steps out of the closet. Being homosexual was a matter of shame until the early 1970s; setting up a "Gay Pride" march turned that on its head. The Pride marches have had their ups and downs but over the years have spread to all parts of the world. Many men of my generation are still afraid of admitting their feelings and live in the shadows as outwardly ordinary family men. Methodist Minister the Reverend Joe Adams recently told his story to BBC Radio Essex which can be found on their website.

One group who still have battles to fight are transsexuals. **"The Extraordinary Life of April Ashley"** (Channel 4) told us the struggles she had growing up in Liverpool, biologically male, but psychologically female. She travelled to Paris to join a transvestite dance club entertaining such people as Omar Sharif and Winston Churchill. She heard of ground-breaking reassignment surgery and went to Casablanca to become the seventh pioneering patient. Ashley recalled rejoicing as she woke up, knowing that her body had been reshaped. A marriage to a peer led to a messy court case which voided the marriage on the basis that "the Law" still considered Ashley a man. I recently met a trans activist who was a teenager at the time of the case. She was in a male public school and would follow every step of Ashley's life. To her it bought hope, just as the Pride marches have for succeeding generations of young people.

Christians haven't always been at our best as we grapple with sexuality and gender. Certainly, I've found as an evangelical that my "live and let live" approach has not always been acceptable, especially to other evangelicals. Many trans and gay activists immediately reject the church and especially evangelicals. Both ways, it can be a painful experience.

"Long Lost Family" (ITV1) , is an increasingly disturbing programme. As two recent stories unfolded, I became very uncomfortable about the ethical basis for this format. Two adults who were adopted as children wanted to find their natural mother and any siblings. From what was said about the mothers, these were women who were facing the enormous financial pressures and the stigma of clearly dysfunctional relationships. These are the sort of problems that used to be aired and exploited on the very unlamented Jeremy Kyle programme.

Having found out that my father had had another son who wanted to meet me, I know just how upsetting these "discoveries" can be. Thank goodness he didn't turn up with a television crew! Just how much long-term support do these recreated families get from the programme makers? Quite rightly, adoption agencies take great care with these searches for natural mothers.

In **"Long Lost Family",** the links are usually followed through the maternal line. There is no mention of the fathers, who seem to have just disappeared. Two phrases spring to mind: the mother is "left holding the baby"; and, as my Jewish friends say, "It's a wise man who knows his own father." This will end badly, and someone is going to get hurt.

Methodist Recorder, 15th July, 2022

"I'm a Romantic, Sentimental, Traditional Anglican",
meet TV broadcaster, former MP and teddy bear collector
Gyles Brandreth

Gyles Brandreth had spent the day conferring degrees at Chester Cathedral on behalf of the City's University, of which he is Chancellor. That's about a thousand handshakes and several speeches. One honorary graduate had quoted a sentence that had caught Gyles's attention: it was the "do all the good you can" rule attributed to John Wesley. "I'm going to put that on my blog," Gyles told me, with an enthusiasm that has endeared him to millions over half a century.

Despite the gruelling day, he was happy to speak to the **Methodist Recorder** because, among other things, he "loved Charles Wesley's hymns". Gyles often says interesting things about faith, not least in his little book "The Seven Secrets of Happiness', but has never been identified as a high-profile "celebrity believer".

Gyles had a very close encounter with the public expression of faith just after leaving Oxford. In the early 1970s, Lord Longford, a committed Catholic, publisher and prison visitor, set up a "commission" on pornography. He brought together the great and the good of various Christian groups but needed some young people. He thought of Cliff Richard but also of Gyles, who he had met at the Oxford Union and had shared their interest in prison reform. Three or four months later, Lord Longford, Gyles and others connected with the commission visited a live sex show in Copenhagen, accompanied by the tabloid press, who doomed the project with ridicule. Gyles, detached himself from the project.

He quickly recovered and went on to write several books about Scrabble, other board games, puzzles, hosted TV programmes—wearing brightly coloured jumpers— appeared in pantomime, opened a teddy bear museum, and became a regular contestant on BBC Radio 4's "Just a Minute" programme.

But political parties like some "stardust" on their candidates list and Gyles served Chester as their Conservative MP for a five-year term before being swept away in the 1997 New Labour landslide. During those five years, he kept a diary which he published shortly after leaving Parliament. There's lots of fascinating detail, names are dropped by the regiment, confidences broken and bucket loads of humour, as he charts the fall of a government grappling with sleaze, "back to basics" and successive "resets". It's a brilliant read and will be poured over by historians for many years to come. He served as a whip and it became obvious he was the "soft cop" in that brutal environment, perhaps an indication that others could see something special in him.

Gyles's childhood was replete with Christian activity, he explained: "My mother was the daughter of a missionary. My grandmother, a splendid lady, whose parents could not manage her financially, sent her to Canada to be adopted. She was first adopted by the Bishop family and had she stayed with them, she would have been the sister of Billy Bishop VC, DSO, the famous air ace of the

First World War. She left the Bishop family and went to another family who were keen Christians and sent her to the Toronto Bible College. When she was 20, she was sent by the college to India, to convert 'the heathen'. She travelled around India on a donkey, alone, with a Bible, making converts. She eventually married an English-born, Indian Army officer, who became my grandfather.

"My father's side was more conventional, they were Church of England," explained Gyles, but quickly digressed. "My grandmother constantly saw the devil on her shoulder, trying to keep him at bay. I read some of her letters and have always been fascinated by the personification of the devil. One of my most interesting interviews as a journalist was with the Papal Exorcist, a very interesting character, who assured me that the devil spoke Latin, so they were able to converse.

"My parents were very traditional. Till the end of their lives they said their prayers on their knees. The Anglican church was how I was brought up. A touch of the high church and a touch of the evangelical. From an early age, I spent most of my spare time at church. I was a server at St Stephen's church, on the Gloucester Road, the 'boat boy' and I would assist the thurifer wearing a surplus and a ruff. I loved this church and I loved the ritual. It was there that I had one of my first 'celebrity encounters'.

"One Christmas, when I was very small, I was asked to read the lesson at the service of nine carols. Afterwards, an elderly gentleman came to congratulate me and the priest-in-charge asked if I knew who he was? I said 'no' and Father Howard explained he was a very famous poet, T.S. Eliot, who it turned out was a sidesman, later a church warden. He encouraged me to learn 'McCavity The

Mystery Cat'. I loved that church and it was an exciting encounter with T.S. Eliot. That was my high Anglican tradition.

"I was also in the choir at Holy Trinity Brompton, which wasn't evangelical in my day. My main recollection is that I loved being in the choir. We got half-a-crown for singing at weddings and five shillings for funerals. Every week, we would look out through our hands as we prayed to see who the older people were and ask God to take them from us. And God obliged, they fell like flies and we sang at their funerals. Again, I very much enjoyed the ritual, the theatre, of it.

"I really do love churches. I collect churches, I collect cathedrals. As Chancellor of the University of Chester, one of the great joys for me is that our graduation ceremonies take place in Chester Cathedral. I spend days gazing at the magnificent west window. There's something wonderful about being in a building where people have worshipped for a thousand years. So, when it comes to faith, I would say that my faith is wrapped up with what we may call 'the English tradition'. I am just a traditional English person; I go to a church in Barnes, in London, that was there when a Bishop stopped by after signing the Magna Carta. The writer Henry Fielding, the author of Tom Jones, worshipped in this church.

"I go there on a weekly basis to the 8am service on a Sunday morning, where they do 'The Book of Common Prayer'. That is a reflection of what I am about. I love the golden thread of our culture, which very much involves the liturgy, the buildings and I love the beauty of the language. Also, I am very interested in poetry; I've recently published a book about poems which can be learnt by heart. The one thing about poetry is that you don't need to understand every word in a poem. Sometimes poems which you completely understand are not doing their job, there needs to be something elusive about a poem. What I'm saying is that liturgy, which makes everything plain, may not be doing its job properly. I'm a romantic, sentimental traditional Anglican."

Gyles makes it clear that he does not proselytise and admits that he still has great friends, such as Richard Harries, the former Bishop of Oxford, who assist him on his journey to understand the nature of God. He found Harries's book, "The Beauty and the Horror", of particular help.

But whatever his doubts, Gyles is adamant that faith is an important part of human existence, pointing out the psychotherapist Carl Jung believed that the people who found happiness tended to have a faith, to have a spiritual dimension.

"Having a faith can clearly be good for you, I am fascinated by faith, I see the value of faith, I see the value of ritual, of prayer, of communion, of the traditions, but one of my problems when I was a Member of Parliament is that I always agreed with the last person I met, so I don't have very firm or fixed opinions. I wouldn't, as it were, stand alongside Joan of Arc or Martin Luther and say 'I believe' but I certainly believe in the value of belief."

After half a century of making the nation smile, Gyles Brandreth, may not share the doctrines and dogmas of many Christians, but his quiet confidence that he should be in church on a Sunday morning should be an encouragement to us all. Gyles may not yet be a national treasure, but is well on his way to being the nation's slightly eccentric, thoughtful, favourite great-uncle.

Methodist Recorder, 29th July, 2022

Goodbye Neighbours, Hello Newsreader

Last week saw the final instalment of the soap opera **"Neighbours"** (Channel 5) and the first two instalments of **"The Newsreader"** (BBC2). By coincidence, both are based on Melbourne, Australia, and owe a lot to the 1980s. Apart from location, they have little in common.

"Neighbours" launched the careers of Kylie Minogue and Jason Donovan. It made a hero, sometimes a bit battered, out of Harold, the Salvation Army tuba player, portrayed by Ian Smith.

It is set on Ramsey Street in a fictional suburb of Melbourne. It was created in 1985 by Reg Watson, who had previously produced the British soap opera "Crossroads". It was always intended to play in both the Australian and British markets and was aimed at the 'teatime' audience. It has since been sold to sixty other countries. The BBC located it between the children's programming on CBeebies and the subversive "Simpsons", making it a must-watch for several generations of teenagers. The storylines were usually quite anodyne, though occasionally stretching into controversy. Latterly, it has been aired on Channel 5, but expect continuous repeats on Freeview and satellite TV.

The first episodes of **"The Newsreader"** have rightly caught a lot of attention, especially the brilliant role of Helen Norville, played by Anna Torv, the newscaster anchor struggling to get the recognition her talents deserve. The depiction of a newsroom in the 1980s—with the swearing, bullying, sexism, impossible deadlines and chase for ratings— encapsulates the working practices of the time. There were no mobile phones, no internet, no computers and few restraints, yet somehow it's believable that Helen would be back on air presenting a major breaking news story a few hours after taking an overdose.

The first series went out in Australia last year, and a second is in production. The entire first series is now on iPlayer, so may make a great binge watch for those who have missed the first episodes.

Far away from the world of deadlines and work, I recently enjoyed Choral Evensong at St Mary's Church, Henley-on-Thames. It was only the third time I had ever attended that form of evening worship. The twenty or so choristers and the organist performed some beautiful music. So, when my favourite historians appeared on TV in **"Lucy Worsley: Elizabeth I's Battle for God's Music"** (BBC4) the following week, I was an interested viewer.

As with much of our culture, Choral Evensong emerged as a compromise following Henry VIII's bitter but much-needed split from Rome. One of the first outcomes was the suppression of the use of Latin plainchant. The brief reigns of Edward VII and Mary were characterised by persecution and suspicion. Queen Elizabeth, keen to secure her throne, chose not to want "windows" into people's souls, and sought a compromise that would be acceptable to all. Choral Evensong, sung in English, was one of those compromises. So, if ever you are in Henley-on-Thames on a Sunday afternoon, pop in for the monthly

Choral Evensong, but pause in the churchyard to see the flower-be-decked grave of singer Dusty Springfield.

Meanwhile, **"Choral Evensong"** (Radio 3) has been a regular Wednesday and Sunday afternoon fixture since religious broadcasting first began. More details are in our weekly listings on this page or on BBC Sounds, which provides a website about the programme.

A few weeks back, I asked some questions about the ethics and pastoral responsibility of the programme **"Long Lost Family"** (ITV1) . The programme's press officer came back and assured me that the makers were very aware of such concerns, saying, "The duty of care on 'Long Lost Family' is paramount and undertaken with exceptional seriousness, with procedures having been painstakingly established across the programme's eleven-year history.

"Our team (of a Senior Social Worker, the Adoption Support Agency [ASA] and psychologists) provides expert intermediary guidance from start to finish and beyond, which informs and guides the careful and responsibly taken steps in each individual case. Continuing support is offered to everyone who takes part and all our contributors are able to see their film and provide input before the final edit, as we always want to be certain that our contributors feel that they have been fairly represented and supported.

"It is inaccurate to suggest that fathers are not involved in the series. There are many examples of programmes in which fathers have been central to searches. Where fathers are absent or don't appear on camera, every effort is made to contact them and inform them of the programme, but, sometimes, they ask for anonymity. "Long Lost Family" is very proud of the record it has built in responding to a fundamental desire among many people in our society, which is to discover more about their identities and reunite with their family members."

Property programmes are not my usual beat but one of our former church members at City Road Methodist Church, in Birmingham, was on **"A Place in the Sun"** (More 4) searching for a retirement home with her sister in the Dordogne. They had a budget of £350,000 and were offered several houses each with up to nine bedrooms, swimming pools and acres of land. Eventually, they settled for a pair of pleasant, but modest bungalows, with their own swimming pools. It seemed a long way from our inner-city church. But as we say, "Once a City Roader, always a City Roader", so perhaps a pastoral visit is due! It would certainly beat Bognor.

Methodist Recorder, 5th August, 2022

Brum's 'Golden Decade' starts with the Commonwealth Games

Wow! Being in the midst of a TV festival of sport is a bit of a whirlwind. Did we see the diving and cricket for real or was it on the telly? Was it the closing or opening ceremony where the Bull appeared, or both? And who'd ever think that the Queen's baton relay would change runners right outside our front door? So much in so few days.

Just seven months ago, Liam Byrne, MP for Hodge Hill, predicted that Birmingham and the West Midlands could be on the cusp of a "Golden Decade". The success of **"The Commonwealth Games"** (BBC1, BBC2 and BBC3) shows that the region can achieve excellence and a Golden Decade is possible. There is already talk of Birmingham hosting Ukraine's Eurovision song contest next year and the massive coverage of the last few weeks will help secure much-needed inward investment.

The sheer scale of the Games is breathtaking: seventy-two countries, five thousand athletes, competing for two hundred and eighty-three medals at fifteen venues. They are supported by thirteen thousand volunteers, three thousand police and watched by a million spectators.

When the West Midlands was first mooted as the venue for the Commonwealth Games, way back in the 1970s, it was almost dismissed out of hand, even ridiculed. My friend, Councillor Steve Eling, worked hard to land the £73 million state-of-the-art Aquatic Centre in Sandwell and got a lot of abuse on social media for his achievement. Then, once the Games became reality, everyone wanted to be part of it! There was a scramble for tickets, thousands made their way to Centenary Square to see the Bull from the opening ceremony, and even I contributed by being part of a team distributing Bibles to the cheerful spectators, which was really special.

However, most of the 2.4 billion people who make up the Commonwealth won't be able to enjoy the vibe in the West Midlands, and we must take our hats off to the BBC. They provided, and distributed, live feeds from every event with summary programmes at least twice a day. The wonders of iPlayer enabled the creation of seven additional channels which were available live or still available as catch-up. For all of our criticism of our national broadcaster, some of which makes its way onto this page, we need to remember that only an organisation with the infrastructure, expertise and personnel would be able to mount such an exercise. Please remember this when you pay your licence fee, or hear politicians attacking the BBC.

For those of us in England, the icing on the cake must have been the **"Women's Euro 2022 Final"** (BBC1). It wasn't part of the Games but watching the Lionesses battle for gold had more than seventeen million four hundred thousand of us on the edge of our seats. Women's sport is now very much on the map and will give a massive fillip to healthier lifestyles and participation.

With a lot of television time taken up by sport, it has been well worth switching on the wireless as an alternative. My highlight was **"Book of the Week: Takeaway Stories from a Childhood behind the Counter"** (BBC Radio 4). Angela Hui and her two brothers were brought up by their parents, originally from Hong Kong, in Beddau, a former mining village in Wales and "sleepynowheresville".

All of Angela's family worked unbelievably long hours to run a takeaway called "Lucky Star", so called because it was opened on one of the luckiest days ever: 8 August 1988. She remembers working from the age of eight shelling the prawns, putting lids on foil containers and taking orders, all whilst trying to do her homework. She had to face sexually abusive telephone calls and the causal racism dressed up as humour typical of the British, even the Welsh. We hear very little from our Chinese community and this programme offers an insight that many may find helpful. It's on BBC Sounds for another fortnight, and the book is available online.

There's one hidden gem tucked away in the schedules which is well worth either getting up at six on a Sunday morning or staying up for late on the repeat on Sunday evening. **"Something Understood: This is My Vigil"** (Radio 4) looks at the hope, fears and endurance from keeping a vigil. Dr Sheila Cassidy reflects on her time as a prisoner in Chile and the vigils she has kept with families as their loved ones have slipped away. This will be helpful to others who struggle with the hopes and fears of waiting and watching. It's also on BBC Sounds for another fortnight.

"The Fight for Saturday Night" (BBC4) introduced by Michael Grade, charts the story of how the TV channels have competed over the years for the prestigious and, in the case of commercial television, profitable Saturday evening peak time television audiences. He tells the inside story of such programmes as, "The Generation Game", "Who wants to be a Millionaire" and "Strictly Come Dancing". It's a fascinating story of skulduggery, real professionalism and supersized egos.

But when I'm stuck at home on a Saturday evening, I tune into **"Not Going Out"** (Dave). Lee Mack plays a very dysfunctional father and husband who gets into all sorts of scrapes, which upsets his family, the in-laws and the neighbours. I love it because it's completely unbelievable. My wife hates it, I'm sure the Lee Mack character reminds her of someone. I can't think who.

Methodist Recorder, 12th August, 2022

The Indian Summer
of freedom, violence, hate and hope

Last weekend, India and Pakistan celebrated 75 years of independence and it was instructive what our TV and radio stations chose to highlight for that anniversary. **"India 1947: Partition in Colour"** (Channel 4) told the miserable story of the final few months of the British Raj. The Viceroy, Lord Mountbatten, worked with the leaders of the two main factions led by Mohammed Ali Jinnah, who demanded a separate Muslim state, and Pandit Nehru, who wanted a united secular state. Using newly-colourised film, the focus was on the dysfunctional relationship between the three leaders as it played out against rising tensions between the religious groups across the soon-to-be-divided country. None of the parties were prepared for the inter-communal violence that would see mass murder, rape and forced migration. This contrasted with the carefully choreographed ceremonies of smart soldiers and fine words provided for the cameras.

"Seven Days in Summer: Countdown to Partition" (BBC4) used archive eye-witness accounts to paint an even grimmer picture. In some places, such as Lahore, with a three-way split between Muslims, Hindus and Sikhs, rival gangs went from house to house looking for anyone, whatever their age, to butcher. Young women were singled out to be raped; others were given the option of forced conversion. This was as a white British barrister, who had never previously visited the country, drew the new borders of the two states. Whilst there were stories of disgusting brutality, there were stories of people protecting others of another faith from the mobs.

Together with **"My Family, Partition and Me: India 1947"** (BBC4) the events of that year are almost presented as a justification of British rule, with the racist undertone that dark-skinned people need British colonialists to stop them killing one another. An alternative view came from a surprising source, with Michael Portillo in **"Great Indian Railway Journeys: Lucknow to Kolkata"** (BBC2). This episode started in Uttar Pradesh, where my mother was born, and told the story of the exploitative and insensitive rule of the East India Company. This led to the bloodshed of the Indian Mutiny and the British dispensing with the East India Company and turning the entire sub-continent into a colony, our "Jewel in the Crown", albeit with the continuing insensitivity. Further on his journey he reveals how the East India Company industrialised opium production, which it exported to China at great profit. On arrival in Kolkata (formerly Calcutta) Portillo explains how massed-produced Lancashire cotton goods displaced local industry. The Indians, of whatever faith, had good reason to want rid of British rule.

"Dangerous Borders: A Journey across India and Pakistan" (BBC4) chronicles the visits of two British-based journalists to the two countries which emerged from partition. One was from an Indian family and lived in Reading, the other from a Pakistan family now in Burnley. The first discovery is that the border created by partition is still a solid division of the two countries and continues to be a source of permanent tension. Other discoveries include a near-secret fashion show in Pakistan, the continued exploitation of the Dalits in secular India and the realisation that there is little hope of the two countries living in peace.

"Inheritors of Partition" (Radio 4) offered much more hope, with the stories of families who had been torn apart by partition. Two moments are especially moving: one man found the village where his grandfather had been protected from the mob seventy-five years ago. He was taken to the former family home, kissed the ground and then hugged the grandson of the man who had saved his grandparents; a young woman, about to marry, was given a carefully preserved sari from her grandmother, having assumed that in her community, saris had never been worn by women. If talk of partition depresses you, this is the perfect antidote on BBC Sounds. But for future anniversaries, it would be good to hear more about the positives of modern India and Pakistan.

We all suffer varying degrees of grief in our lives. In churches, we often find ourselves asked to help others as they grieve, especially if we are asked to help with funerals. Frankly, we all find bereavement difficult and each of us manages, or otherwise, in different ways. So, it was with considerable interest that I switched on to see **"Good Grief with Reverend Richard Coles"** (Channel 4). Richard's partner died a few years back and he is still trying to cope with his loss. He frequently refers to his status as a vicar, at one point even sitting in his boxer shorts wearing a clerical collar, but only in the last few minutes does he refer to the Christian mystery of faith and hope. Meanwhile, he takes us on a giddy tour of wacky ways to get out more and make new friends, some of which, to be honest, seemed to be open to exploitation. Be wary of recommending this programme to someone coping with bereavement unless you have seen it first.

Sadly, we can't all get to the Edinburgh fringe to see Jon Culshaw's acclaimed "Flying High" where he recreates the brilliance of Les Dawson. Dawson's humour was of its time, but is now being appreciated by a younger audience. If you want to smile after reading this uncharacteristically sad review, catch up with **"Les Dawson: 30 Funniest Moments"** (Channel 5). It will make you laugh. Promise.

Methodist Recorder, 19th August, 2022

Social Media:
the life raft and the ship wreck

During lockdown, very many of us discovered the benefits of social media. We were able to keep in touch with friends and family, participate in worship and even join choirs. For most of us, it was a life raft.

Three recent TV programmes show a different story. One father complained to a true crime documentary that if it weren't for social media, his murdered son would be alive today; another teenager of about the same age became the victim of a dangerous app; and a third related the complex story of a university lecturer who tried to create a new personality in her search for emotional fulfilment.

"Who You Think I Am" (BBC4) is a superb film by Safy Nebbou based on Camille Lauren's bestseller. Claire, played by Juliette Binoche, is a divorced lecturer in her 50s who has been let down in love. She is obviously very confident in her university role, but her emotional life is a mess. The story is told using flashbacks from Claire's sessions with a psychotherapist, another middle-aged woman, played by Nicole Garcia, who clearly has her own emotional issues and asks Claire directly if social media is a life raft or a shipwreck.

After an argument with Ludo, who clearly sees their sexual relationship as a convenient detail, Claire creates a fake Facebook profile for a twenty-four-year-old model called "Clara" to make contact with Ludo's much younger colleague and friend, with whom she unintentionally falls in "love". She then has to grapple with being a fifty-year-old woman but the object of affection as a twenty-four-year-old.

From one or two friends, I know this is not as far-fetched as it seems. Social media offers opportunities to create personas which are far from reality. The film is ninety-five minutes long, is in French with subtitles and on iPlayer for another eleven weeks. There are scenes and language of a sexual nature and it is probably best avoided by anyone recovering from recent emotional upset.

"The Murder of Alex Rodda: Social Media Murders" (ITV1) is billed as the tragic story of a fifteen-year-old boy who was murdered "by a man who had groomed him online". Online grooming does happen; just last year a sixty-year-old man I know was ambushed live on Facebook by a vigilante group who disrupted his efforts to meet with a teenage girl. Alex's "grooming" does not fall neatly into the same category. He was open about his sexuality and had built up a following on Instagram, Snapchat and TikTok with videos of his singing and dancing. His parents were well aware of his exposure but didn't seem to appreciate the unwanted attention such a high profile could bring. The "man" who groomed him, was a nineteen-year-old former classmate of Alex's sister. He wanted a homosexual liaison but not exposure as gay. Somehow, the nineteen-year-old paid Alex over £2,000 for silence. Didn't both sets of parents notice that their sons were involved in a transaction of that size? This happened in a small northern English town. The two could have met at a Young Farmers dance and the outcome could have been the same. We need to alert our children to the dangers life can bring, be it online or in person.

Another northern English town provides the backdrop to the fictitious **"Red Rose"** (BBC3). This young adult drama follows Rochelle—played by Isis Hainsworth—after she accepts an invitation to a mysterious app on her mobile phone. Here, again, social media is the channel for her problems, not the cause.

Nicola Walker and Sean Bean make a convincing middle-aged suburban married couple in Stefan Golaszwski's new drama series, **"Marriage"** (BBC1). Several critics thought the first episode slow and uninspiring, one even complaining that it was like "watching paint dry". After thirty-four years of marriage, I could see what Golaszwski was driving at: marriage is a wonderfully complex relationship where all our emotions, irritations, actions, fears, anxieties, hopes, disappointment, joys, tragedies and habits are on display to at least one other person. At church, at work, at the club and on social media, we can put on all manner of personas but in marriage, no pretence can last forever. If you aren't already hooked on this series, it's worth watching the first episode on iPlayer. But beware: if you are married, some of the scenes are a bit like looking in the mirror.

This week's radio pick must be **"The Food Programme Fried Chicken: a Story of Race and Identity"** (Radio 4). I wish I had heard this programme when I joined City Road Methodist Church way back in the 1980s. We enjoyed some brilliant fried chicken cooked by members of our "Windrush generation" congregation. We took it a bit for granted. Sadly, there is a political story here which harks back to the days of slavery, and explains why West African and Caribbean cuisine have similarities but also sharp differences. It's still on BBC Sounds and well worth a listen.

When I was a child in an East London working-class area, many of my friends' fathers kept pigeons. Now I don't know a single fancier. Apparently, there are far fewer fanciers than just a few years back. The story of our love affair with these birds is told in **"Flights of Fancy: Pigeons and the British"** (BBC4). It's a brilliant reminder of recent working-class history and a great nostalgic watch.

Methodist Recorder, 26th August, 2022

Diana Was Pursued
by the media in both life and death

One evening in 1980 I had supper with the very distressed proprietor of a kindergarden in Kensington. A member of her staff, Diana Spencer, still a teenager, was the target of media interest and being tipped as a future wife for Prince Charles, the heir to throne. The story she told was appalling: basically, every member of staff, parent and child at the nursery was under siege from very rude and pushy photographers.

As a public relations officer, I was keen to know what support the poor woman was getting from the Palace. "Absolutely none" was the stark reply. By December, Diana's exasperated mother wrote a heartfelt letter to The Times, asking the media to lay off. It wasn't until a formal engagement was announced in February 1981 that the Palace offered any official support and protection.

Seventeen years later, that support and protection had been long withdrawn and Diana lay dying in a Paris underpass, still pursued by the media as she took her last breaths. That was twenty-five years ago this week and then what followed was one of the most extraordinary weeks many of us can recall. On the day of her death, I bought, and still have, the Sunday newspapers which had the wrap-around four pages, "tributes", with the tragic news. On the inside pages are the nasty vitriol and intrusive photographs that had been prepared the previous week.

This anniversary has attracted considerable media attention. On Wednesday evening, **"Diana"** (ITV1) promised to reveal "the real woman behind the glamorous media image, recounting some key moments in her remarkable journey from teenage nursery assistant to princess, fashion icon and global star". A three-part series in August, the **"Diana's Decades"** (ITV3) traced her life across the 1970s, 80s and 90s. On the whole, this series focused on the positive side of her life, especially her openness to many people previously shunned and shamed, such as HIV/AIDS patients and those facing mental health challenges. Diana was undoubtedly a star, and I know from my work with Methodism's own National Children's Home how much we would have liked her to have been involved with our organisation.

Sadly, her relationship with Prince Charles did not survive as the age gap and their very different attitudes took their toll. After years of sniping through the media, Diana was interviewed in 1995 by BBC journalist Martin Bashir and made the comment that there were three people in her marriage—including Camilla Parker-Bowles. **"The Diana Interview: the Truth behind the Scandal"** (Channel 4) first seen in 2020, updated in 2021, tells the sorry tale of the tactics used by Bashir to secure the infamous interview. By that time, Diana had learnt to be wary of those who sought her attention or worked for her. Bashir allegedly spotted this insecurity and fear, using it to manipulate Diana into giving the interview. Whilst Bashir's tactics may have been wrong, there is no doubt that Diana had, for many years, been keen to tell her side of the story, as we had already seen with the iconic photo session of her alone at the Taj Mahal in 1992.

It does seem that Diana found happiness, and some security, when she started a relationship with Dodi Fayed, son of the Egyptian owner of Harrods. This enraged the British establishment and in the weeks leading to her death, much media coverage was near-racist. The four part **"Investigating Diana: Death in Paris"** (Channel 4) was a painstaking review of the accident which killed her and Dodi in Paris, along with many conspiracy theories, and the efforts by both French and British police to get to the truth. During those months, the British media portrayed the French police as unprofessional and uninterested. A similar dismissiveness was observable towards the Portuguese police following the disappearance of Madelaine McCann ten years later. However, the interviews with members of the *Brigade Criminelle*, revealed a professionalism, detachment and commitment which was both compelling to see and reassuring.

Just as an aside, readers may not be aware that Dodi Fayed, played a key, though controversial role, in financing the Oscar-winning 1981 film "Chariots of Fire", which tells the story of Christian athlete Eric Liddell at the 1924 Olympics. It's well worth a first or second look, though currently only on subscription services.

It is disappointing that the turmoil within the royal family as Diana and Charles's marriage unwound now seems to be repeating itself in the family's relationship with their son, Harry, and his wife, Meghan. Predictably, the Duchess of Sussex has come in for a lot of criticism following the release of her first podcast **"Archetypes"** (Spotify). It wasn't quite my sort of thing, but

I don't think Meghan deserved to be panned by the British press as she has been in the last week. It is free to listen, but you will have to create a Spotify account, again for free.

If you want to go completely off-beat, the 1957 adaptation of Agatha Christie's **"Witness for the Prosecution"** (BBC2) will be on iPlayer for just another fortnight. A brilliant plot, a peep into the 1950s, and amazing acting by Marlene Dietrich, Tyrone Power and Charles Laughton, whose attitude to women certainly needs updating. The story isn't over until an announcement at the end implores the viewer not to tell others who may want to see it for themselves. My lips are sealed.

Methodist Recorder 2nd September, 2022

As the Nights Draw in, the coppers are looking for the villains

New detective dramas will certainly darken our evenings as the nights draw in. Three new series all arrive at the same time, two with interesting twists and a third, which is very familiar.

Let's start with a fallen heart-throb. Captain Ross Poldark proved to be a friend of the Methodists when he protected them during the turbulent years following the American and French revolutions. Aidan Turner played the heroic captain with distinction. Although there may still be mileage in the Poldark saga, Turner returns to our screens as **"The Suspect"** (ITV). This is a full-on psychological drama, with Turner's new character, Joe O'Loughlin, paying a successful psychologist with a loving family and recently lauded as a hero after a stunt opener which would be worthy of a Bond movie.

However, all is not well. Despite only being in his mid-forties, he has recently been diagnosed with an early onset of Parkinson's syndrome and we see details of how he tries to cope with the practicalities and emotions of the condition. A little later, we find out that a few years before, O'Loughlin had faced some professional difficulties following a complaint by a patient. The police asked him to provide some help to profile the possible perpetrator of a particularly horrific murder. There then follows a series of coincidences and questions which begin to show him in an unflattering light. Not so much as a whodunnit as a "did-he-do-it?". Great acting, original story and lots of intrigue. I'm hooked and will certainly watch the rest of the series. Oh, watch out for Cara, played by Bronagh Waugh, who is mentioned elsewhere in this column.

If you have doubts about all those CCTV cameras all over the place and facial recognition and personal data, then the new series of **"The Capture"** (BBC 1) will do nothing to reassure you. Just what happens when the Chinese are bidding to provide a very high specification facial recognition system for the British Border Force? We see surveillance technology meeting artificial intelligence with dramatic and unforeseen consequences. Holliday Grainger plays Rachel Carey, a frustrated detective constable. It is difficult to work out which side she is on. There are signs that she may be going rogue. Lots of spooky background music with shadows and lights around soulless modern buildings. This is the second series so must have following, but it didn't hold my interest and I won't be watching it again.

Maverick detectives are always a feature of TV crime drama and **"Ridley"** (ITV1) is no exception. Adrian Dunbar, previously known as Superintendent Ted Hastings in "Line of Duty", plays Alex Ridley, who had been granted "access to pension on medical grounds" following the deaths of his wife and daughter in a fire. Ridley had taken to drink, left cases unsolved, and sunk into despair, though he has some good friends who look out for him. Then a local farmer is shot on his way home from the pub.

Detective Inspector Carol Farman, also played by Bronagh Waugh, has taken the promotion following Ridley being pensioned off. She does a great job of working through her "imposter syndrome" and eventually asks for Ridley's help, first unofficially but then on a temporary basis for this one case. She and Ridley make a great team, with her professionalism and his experience piecing together a really nasty story that could have provided a happy ending, but left us wondering. **"Ridley"** has all the hallmarks of a police murder mystery drama: scene of crime tents and tape, emotionally detached pathologists, plus friction between official procedure and old fashioned corner cutting. The heroes could be Morse, Vera or even Father Brown. Each story will be self-contained, so no need to check the listings for the next episode in case you miss something. **"Ridley"** will come back for at least another three or four series and then forever on Freeview and streaming services. Ideal viewing with the late-night cocoa.

We're just a week away from the next series of "Strictly Come Dancing", so I thought it worth getting a little more background by watching **"Blackpool's Dance Fever"** (BBC1). Each year, the Empress Ballroom at the Winter Gardens— previously the home of political party conferences and latterly Methodism's own "Easter People"—turns itself into the venue for the prestigious British Open Ballroom Dancing Championship. Looks can deceive and the professionals make it slick and professional as they glide across the dance floor in smart suits and glamorous frocks. The reality is very different as we follow several couples through the training and build-up to the competition. Quite apart from the arduous practice and "boot camps" overseen by zealous coaches, there's the whole pressure of deciding what to wear. One contestant was delighted to have picked up a dress for just £600 when normally it would have cost £2,500! The dancers spend a lot of time working on their hair and suntan and very little seems to be left to chance. If you enjoy "Strictly", this is well worth a preview catch-up on iPlayer.

My radio pick this week, especially for anyone working with young people, must be **"The Dark Side of Direct Sales"** (Radio 4 FM). It is a helpful warning not to follow the self-employed route. Selling is probably one of the most wonderful things you can do fully clothed, but there are some sharks out there waiting to exploit enthusiastic young people.

Methodist Recorder 9th September, 2022

"Nana" Tells Us all
We Need To Know
with the death of our Queen

My three-year-old son summed it up way back in 1996. We were glued to the Midlands TV news waiting to see the news report of the Queen's visit to my Hereford constituency.

"Nana", he said, as The Queen shook my hand. In that single word, my toddler had summed up the thoughts of the entire Commonwealth. Queen Elizabeth II was a very special person and she may have been our Head of State, but she was much more than that, she was grandmother to the nation.

The late Queen's life and death were led in front of the television cameras. I first saw her Coronation live way back in 1953. There aren't very many people left who can say that. Less than ten per cent of households had a TV set; our house was crowded with friends and neighbours whilst my father hung out of the window waving the aerial because the technology of the day was unreliable.

Last week, more than 69 years later, I stood and—I must admit—shed a tear after Huw Edwards, reported the Buckingham Palace announcement of her death and the national anthem was played. For one last time, we were singing in our hearts "God save our gracious Queen". It was the end of an era, played out in full on our television sets.

Of course, we have always known that Her Majesty would die one day. I worked in a BBC radio station and we even held a rehearsal in readiness for a Royal death; at that point, the Queen Mother. However, when the Queen's death was announced most of us felt a sense of shock. It seemed that she would go on forever. But we know that was not possible.

The first indication came via social media. The bloggers and tweeters had noticed that there were hurried notes, and then a statement as Parliament was being televised. Soon afterwards the TV news channels started bringing updates from Balmoral, Windsor and Buckingham Palace.

Unexpectedly, for such a breaking news story, there seemed to be very few moments when the newsrooms were struggling to bring us updates. There was just so much to say. Then there came a moment, sometime about 4:30pm, when the atmosphere changed. It suddenly felt as if the newsrooms knew something that the rest of us didn't. Once again, turning to social media, there were reports of long faces and black ties being donned at Westminster.

The official announcement came at 6:30pm. The newsreader on ITN seemed a little flustered, almost hesitant, as if she couldn't quite believe the words on her teleprompter. Over on BBC TV Huw Edwards was word perfect as he made the announcement and brought the nation to tears. A few minutes later, we were shown the scene at Buckingham Palace as two footmen fixed a notice to the railings confirming her death. My thoughts went back to my time on BBC local radio; everyone hoped that they would not be on duty when there was a death in the Royal Family.

Then, we started to live the new reality. We learnt that the "The King and Queen Consort" were at Balmoral. Then the Prime Minister gave a subdued tribute during which she referred to "King Charles III". It was the first time I had ever heard anyone say "God save the King", except in old newsreels and films.

All the main terrestrial television channels cancelled programmes and focused on bringing us the tributes from around the world. The BBC radio stations, both national and local, were tuned into a single programme across the network. On the smaller channels, the reaction varied. QVC cancelled all its shopping portals, BBC4 and BBC3 were suspended. Dave, UKTV and Yesterday carried a flash on the screen referring viewers to the main news channels. It was surprising that ITVbe, ITV2 and ITV4 carried on regardless. In these circumstances broadcasters had to make a very careful and sensitive judgement, about which programmes to cancel and for how long.

Obviously, the obituary films had been long planned. It was touching that they had to be updated at the last minute to include photographs of her swearing in her new Prime Minister just a few days before.

As the tributes came into the newsrooms from around the world, it was obvious that these were not stereotype, ready-made copy and paste tributes, but heartfelt expressions of love and affection from the world's leaders, both past and present.

In the following days, we were told the details of her lying in state, the funeral and the length of the formal period of state mourning. In due course, we will know the date of the coronation, a word that dominated my life when I was the same age as my son who exclaimed "Nana".

The Queen's Coronation was the first of a British sovereign to be broadcast to the world. Her funeral will be the first of a British monarch to receive global coverage. Her life was led in front of the cameras with all the opportunities and liabilities that entailed.

Possibly the most moving archive footage played and replayed during that momentous evening was her pledge in 1947 that her whole life whether long or short would be dedicated to serving her people. She fulfilled that promise with interest and, even all those years ago, my toddler immediately recognised her place in our family.

Methodist Recorder, 16th September, 2022

"Strictly" Is Back,
but have ITV already thrown in the towel for Saturday night ratings?

Last autumn, I was on the edge of my seat each Saturday evening hoping to see my pick, Rose Ayling-Ellis, get through to the next round of **"Strictly Come Dancing"** (BBC1) as predicted in this column. Despite the delay, we are all looking for similar excitement in 2022. But what if "Strictly" isn't our thing? What is the opposition offering?

ITV launched its Saturday night schedule in late August and early September, hoping to steal a march on the BBC. But after watching the opening ITV shows, I will stick with "Strictly"! I must ask: has ITV have already thrown in the towel?

ITV is scheduling five consecutive game shows each Saturday over five and a half hours, from 4pm to 10pm, with a welcome half-hour break for news. Of the three that I caught, the formats were contrived, tired and frankly, cheap. There's no drama, no comedy, not even a soap. And in most, there is a focus on "celebrities", many of whom neither you nor I have never heard of.

"Who Wants to be a Millionaire?" (ITV1) now back for its thirty-fourth run is probably the best of the Saturday evening commercial offering. Jeremy Clarkson jollies the contestants along as they work their way through a series of closed-choice questions, in the hope that they can land the £1 million prize. It was a lot of money when the programme was first aired in 1998, but due to rising house prices, bulging pension pots and runaway inflation, the prize pot is beginning to shrink. The tired format looks more suitable for a Wednesday day-time audience than for Saturday night prime time.

At least Clarkson lets the wannabe millionaires bask in the limelight during their moments of fame. The same cannot be said for the "panels" in the two preceding programmes: attention is very firmly fixed on the celebrity judges. **"The Voice UK"** (ITV1) is supposed to provide raw talent, usually newcomers or amateurs, with the opportunity to bid for a recording contract. There were some really good performances from some fine young people. However, the cameras were fixed on the judges as they made their decisions, hands hovering over buttons, gesticulating and grimacing to one another whilst the studio audience shouted and whooped over the singers. There was no sign of a live band and it was little more than a glorified karaoke. The four judges are all well-known singers in their own right: Tom Jones, Olly Murs, Anne-Marie and will.i.am, who seem to be squandering their own talents on this show.

"The Masked Dancer" (ITV1) is even worse, repeat, even worse! Once again the celebrity panel is centre stage. It includes Jonathan Ross, Davina McColl, Oti Mabuse and Peter Crouch. At least in this one they are not chopping up "civilians" but other "celebrities", carefully disguised in ridiculous costumes which cover their faces and reflect their names, such as Candlestick, Scissors, Odd Socks and Prawn Cocktail. It's all carefully scripted with jokes and asides that make a scout troop Gang Show qualify as comedy genius.

The six contestants have a face-off with one another and the studio audience decides who continues and who is consigned to a second round, which leads to one of them being eliminated and unmasked - and the viewer underwhelmed. Seriously, if you are looking for an alternative to "Strictly", channel-surf Freeview or put on the wireless.

Ideally, to give a comprehensive Saturday alternative to "Strictly" we should also review **"Celebrity Lingo"** (ITV1) and **"Ninja Warrior UK: Race for Glory"** (ITV1) but after three hours, I was posted as missing in action. More about "Strictly" soon.

New Yorker John Wilson may be about to deliver a nugget which becomes a niche comedy. His twenty-five minute documentaries are shot as he wanders around the city finding people to speak with. You hear him, but don't see him, and meet a wonderful array of characters apparently picked at random as they too roam around. **"How to with John Wilson"** (BBC2) will see him tackle a series of tasks from covering your own furniture, putting up scaffolding, and how to remember your dreams. He kicked off with how to make small talk, with some very basic tips of how to strike up a conversation (buy a band tee-shirt) what to avoid (weather good, climate change bad) and how to end it (just touch-and-go). Small talk, he says, fills spaces and provides the social glue to keep us together. I wasn't quite certain if this is a humour that would mainly appeal to a certain sort of person, probably men. I liked it. If you missed the first episode, the whole series is already on iPlayer.

The last fortnight has certainly been memorable with the media having to adjust schedules to carry the news surrounding the late Queen's funeral and the King's accession. It is understandable that "Strictly" was cancelled, but surely the **"Last Night of the Proms"** (BBC1) could have been adapted?

Heather Burton's **"DifferentAnglezShow"** (Newstyle) was left without contributors at the last minute so I stepped in for an hour to recall my memories of the Queen, her Coronation and her legacy. It was challenging to speak to a mainly African Caribbean audience whose recollections of our monarchy, both here and in the Caribbean, may have been very different to those of us born in the UK to white British families in post-war Britain.

Methodist Recorder 23rd September, 2022

Ten Days When Time Stood Still
as we mourned our Queen

The actor Felicity Kendall summed it up on the morning of the funeral of Queen Elizabeth II: "For ten days, time has stood still." It certainly felt like that as the final blessing was said by the Archbishop of Canterbury at the close of the comital service at Windsor Castle.

Some of us were able to take part in the events following the Queen's death. We marked it in our churches and civic proclamations were read in many towns and cities. But for most of us, the period of mourning was played out live on our television and radios.

It was absolutely right for the major broadcasters to scrap the planned schedule on the evening the Queen's death was announced. But what happened in the following ten days tells us much about modern Britain, much of it very good, but some of it less flattering.

After ten days of saturation coverage, it was a relief when the service began at Westminster Abbey. The shape of the service, though much shorter, could have come from almost any Methodist chapel in the country. The broadcasters did a superb job focusing on the service, rather than be star struck with cut-in shots of politicians, celebrities or even the Royal Family.

The choice of hymns was comforting and appropriate with "The Day Thou Gavest" reminding us of music and sentiments we have lost as our evening congregations evaporate. "The Lord is my Shepherd" to Crimond remains an all-time favourite for Christian funerals and is still known beyond the walls of our congregations. Given Methodism's turbulent beginnings, it was good that Charles Wesley's hymn "Love Divine", which many of us associate with weddings, brought the theology together.

The Archbishop of Canterbury's sermon, stressing Her Majesty's sense of duty and commitment, may have been uncomfortable for some, but needed to be said. The readings were challenging and well worth making a focus for our own quiet times during periods of grieving: I Corinthians 15:20-26, 53-58; Psalm 42: 1-7; and John 14:1-9a. It was good to see our own Helen Cameron and Graham Thompson taking part, though many of us may have been caught off-guard by seeing them described as "Reverend Canon".

In terms of television coverage of such an event, we do need to ask a fundamental question: Is the Abbey, with its complex division into nave, quire, transept and sanctuary really the best setting for such an event? Perhaps for next year's Coronation, the Palace should look at either Methodist Central Hall or even the Queen Elizabeth II Conference Centre, both within a couple of hundred yards of the Abbey.

But there are also some more controversial questions. Cremation without ceremony is the fastest growing sector in the British funeral market, and it is worth pausing to ask whether such a long drawn out series of commemorations, with extended news programmes and, frankly, some tedious live coverage from helicopters, is really in keeping with how we mourn these days? I conducted a funeral during one of those ten days. It had taken a fortnight for the family to get the death certificate and another three weeks to find a half-hour slot at a crematorium. In the intervening five weeks, the family had to get on with their lives.

The queue for the laying in state at Westminster Hall was unnecessary in the modern age. It was almost turned it into a macho reality game, with claims that some people would have to wait up to twenty-two hours. Even a trip to our local council tip in Oldbury has to be booked online. Surely it would have been more respectful to the late Queen to have had such a booking system? Night after night of TV "vox pops" from the queue just helped make the whole thing look like a circus. News from Ukraine, where fighting was escalating, was reduced to a two-minute mention at the end of each of the extended bulletins.

The nadir was surely reached on the Thursday before the funeral, when a Radio 4 afternoon news bulletin was led by the "news" that the Queen's coffin would be drawn on a gun carriage by 142 naval ratings. Since 1901, when Victoria died, that has always been the case, so why was it a lead story on a news bulletin?

What may have been more newsworthy, as we found out on the day of the funeral, is that of the 142 naval ratings, many of them only recently recruited, not one of them was Black or Asian. We showed to the world that there is still a job to be done in celebrating diversity in our armed forces.

I spent some time watching the live coverage on French TV, it was beautifully done with captions, respectful commentary and simultaneous translation. However, they did ask the question: how much did this cost? Four thousand five hundred military personnel were taken off their normal jobs and scores of police were on overtime.

Then there were the uniforms, at times more like costumes: so many different sorts with expensive embroidery and braiding. How is all this maintained for events which happen just once or twice in a generation? Was such a long parade really necessary? It would have much better if the Royal Family had been left to mourn in their own way once the service at the Abbey had been concluded. Not everything has to be on television.

Methodist Recorder 30th September, 2022

Time for a Little Sauce
and lots of sparkle

We all know what an awful autumn we are having, but on Friday nights there is a real gem of a programme to cheer us all up. If you have missed the first couple of episodes, catch up on My5 at any time of the week, especially when things get really dim and dismal.

"From Paris to Rome with Bettany Hughes" (Channel 5) is a travel programme like no other. Bettany actually knows what she is talking about, being something of an evangelist of arts, history and classics for the masses. A graduate of St Hilda's, Oxford, and a university lecturer, Bettany has a way of conveying lots of information in an accessible and friendly way. At times, she can be, well, a little saucy.

Her series opened with a visit to Paris. Bettany believes that good food and drink, coupled with interesting company and inspiring culture, can really lift the soul. She agrees with Audrey Hepburn that "Paris is always a good idea". In the first thirty minutes she explains the Enlightenment, tells us what a restaurant is and describes the Venus de Milo in a way that gently increases the blood pressure.

After the understandable delay following the Queen's death, **"Strictly Come Dancing"** (BBC 1) is well and truly back on a Saturday evening with lots of fun and acres of sparkle. On Sunday night, we have the results and dance off, which I'm sure is recorded at about 10pm the previous evening.

Sadly, there has been some criticism of this series because there's not a "big-name"celebrity and a feeling that the choice of contestants is a little "woke". For those who do not feed into the right-wing national press, "woke" is what used to be known as "political correctness"; there's always a trope with these people. The main objection seems to be that Richie Anderson and Giovanni Pernice are dancing together. In so many other cultures, same sex groups and couples dance together. It is insulting to suggest that dancing together implies a sexual relationship. And why shouldn't Paralympic swimmer Ellie Simmonds enjoy a good dance? Last year, Rose Ayling-Ellis showed us what a deaf person can do. Perhaps we should have more "woke"contestants?

But the clouds on the horizon can't keep off our screens for long. **"1978: Winter of Discontent"** (Channel 5) took us back to the period between November 1978 and February 1979 when the country felt as if it was falling apart. Inflation and a government-imposed cap on pay rises led to a breakdown in industrial relations. Contributors included Esther Rantzen and Alastair Stewart, who drew menacing parallels with our current gathering crisis. Saturday night TV was then dominated by Esther Rantzen's programme "That's Life", which, thankfully, I rarely watched because as a bachelor in my twenties, I was out on the razzle. I just wonder if in forty-three year's time TV commentators will chide us for enjoying "Strictly" as the world fell apart.

"I bet you won't watch **"The Labour Files"** (Al Jazeera)" said someone I met at a fringe meeting during a recent party conference. Well, actually I have—all three episodes. I even know some of the people and something of the incidents featured in the programme. It purports to "expose" how the Labour Party dealt with a large number of people who, frankly, joined to disrupt the party and often spouted anti-Semitism. Much of it was based on stolen documents, surrounding various disciplinary cases. Those who have dealt with discipline at work or in the church will know how fraught that can be. My memories of the Corbyn years (and Jeremy was not implicated) is of being threatened with disciplinary action because I raised a safeguarding concern and separately seeing a good local councillor suspended just days before his re-selection so that he could not be considered. **"The Labour Files"** is dishonest propaganda.

When Jean and Stewart had baby Jessica in the 1980s, I prayed a silent prayer that she would grow big and strong and care for those around her, as I always do for newborns. **"File on Four: Isobel's Story"** (Radio 4) brought me close to tears as the plight of British victims of sex trafficking was described in detail. Somehow, radio is a much better medium for such a story than print or TV. Jessica had two wonderful loving parents and was fortunate not to go through the pain and trauma that confronted Isobel as she grew up, exploited and used during her teenage years. Sadly, her cries for help were ignored until Labour MP Jess Phillips took up her case. My prayers all those years ago for Jessica were answered, as they are every time Jess speaks about domestic violence and abuse. Don't be afraid of big prayers for the smallest baby.

"The Absolutely Fabulous June Whitfield" (Channel 5) celebrated a brilliant actor who managed to re-invent herself over nearly seventy years. Some older readers may remember her as the Eth Glum in the radio show "Take it From Here". Many more of us will remember her brilliant jousting with Tony Hancock as the blood donor nurse in "Hancock's Half Hour". June took joint top billing in the long running sit-com "Terry and June" which focused on the rather boring life of a 1980s suburban couple. Then, finally, it's the 1990s glamour and champers in "Absolutely Fabulous". Cheer yourself up, catch up on My5.

Methodist Recorder 14th October, 2022

How Self-Esteem and Music
make for good mental health
and well-being

Every now and then a TV programme can offer an unexpected challenge. **"Ten Years Younger in Ten Days"** (Channel 5) may easily be dismissed as another makeover programme, but the current series also includes a follow-up of those who were advised a couple of years back. It certainly leads to questions about how we perceive ourselves and are seen by others.

Three people had been through the ten-day process and lived to tell the tale. Myrah had gone from a "frumpy" (her word) looking fifty-six-years-old, to looking a cool thirty-nine-years-old much younger than her real age of forty-five. She is enthusiastic as she described the change it made to her life, making her feel both physically and mentally healthier.

"Biker" Tom had started with a shaggy beard, long hair, both adorned by scruffy tee-shirts and ill-fitting trousers. His makeover took him to the barbers for a shave, Saville Row for a decent suit, the dentist for some teeth whitening and even a make-up artist to advise on the use of some non-obtrusive make-up. He got a promotion and has now set his sights on an even better job.

Klara is a lollipop lady who wore baggy clothes, had spotty skin and saw herself as an "ugly duckling". Some coaching about how to appreciate her body shape when choosing clothes, a new hairdo, and "micro-needling" to sort out her spots made a dramatic transformation. She, too, reported that the makeover was just the start of a process about how she felt about herself.

All three were convinced that some very simple changes to their appearance had boosted their self-esteem, which helped with their confidence both at work and at leisure. We Christians often have mixed feelings about spending time and money on making ourselves look good. We certainly steer clear of pride and displays of wealth, but there's no reason we shouldn't try to look and feel our best.

Self-esteem and pride was a massive factor in **"Our Dementia Choir Sings Again with Vicky McClure"** (BBC1). Some find dementia "early stages" and "senior moments" a source of humour, but as we get older and see our friends succumb we begin to wonder whether we will be next. It's a very distressing one-way street. Vicky McClure believes that music therapy can have a positive impact by reducing anxiety, depression and agitation. She brought together a group of dementia sufferers to record a single at the Abbey Road studio in London.

This programme was an emotional roller coaster but it was so inspiring to see people, each with very different histories, face the challenge of working and singing together. It was lovely to share the pride felt by the relatives and carers as they enjoyed the choir practise and perform, they too benefited. Churches, especially Methodist churches, are one of the few places where people can sing on a weekly basis. Could we consciously encourage dementia sufferers and their families to join us each week? It could be a new witness, and we're singing anyway, so funding is not an issue.

"Music Matters" (Radio 3) ran a special edition in advance of World Mental Health day which looked at the benefits of music to those coping with health issues. We are reminded that we all have a right to make music and have the power to communicate through song and sound. It's on BBC Sounds, so worth a listen by anyone seeing music as a medium to help improve mental health.

One real source of low self-esteem for many women is the bodily changes which take place during the menopause. The World Health Organisation now recognises that very few women, and virtually no men, understand the menopause. So, October has been declared World Menopause Month. TV presenter Cherry Healey explained many of the issues to **"Laura Crompton"** (BBC Radio Manchester) not least of which was that women are belittled by being told they are "over the hill" and just have mild depression or "brain fog". This often leads to misdiagnosis in the medical sphere and missed promotions at work. The health food retailer Holland and Barrett are offering special help, so it may be worth a visit to their bigger stores. This programme will be on BBC Sounds for another fortnight.

I don't like true-life murder dramas. I watched **"Maxine"** (Channel 5) because it was about the 2002 Soham murders of two ten-year old girls. One of the police officers on the case was my godson, who, I found out later, discovered critical evidence which helped put the murderer, Ian Huntley, behind bars. Huntley evaded suspicion for several days because his partner, Maxine Carr, provided a false alibi. This programme showed how low self-esteem can have fatal results. Huntley both loved and loathed Carr whilst always wanting to be in control. Maxine clearly needed love and recognised that Huntley, despite his faults, could provide some semblance of the love that she craved. It's only twenty years since these horrific murders, there's no suggestion of a miscarriage of justice or an appeal for more witnesses, so why was this programme even made?

If you want a TV free evening, Google "The Syrian Baker Farnham Maltings". It is a wonderful play touring much of the country. It would make a great TV or radio drama. Go and see it. You see someone find their self-esteem and help others among the ruins of war.

Methodist Recorder 21st October, 2022

Fifty Years of Radio 4's
'Thought for the Day'

BBC Radio 4's **"Thought for the Day"** broadcast each morning, shortly before 8am, can seem a quiet few minutes of reflection at the start of a busy day, an opportunity to use the loo, or a challenge to long-cherished beliefs. Speaking straight into a microphone "live" often with a script that has been changed or rewritten to reflect a breaking new story, gives each talk an edge which is often lacking in pre-recorded broadcasting.

"Thought" started way back in 1970 when the BBC recast Radio 4's morning schedule as a rolling news programme rather than the previous, more static, format. They inherited "Lift Up Your Hearts", which even then seemed dated and a little too earnest. Renamed as "Thought for the Day", this precious slot has become a favourite of listeners from all faiths and two years ago celebrated its golden anniversary.

Christine Morgan edited the slot for ten years and then went on to become Head of Religion and Ethics for BBC Radio, which meant she clocked up thirty-three years working on "Thought". She has bought together a sample of those talks in **"Thought for the Day, Fifty Years of Inspiring Thoughts and Reflections"** (BBC Books). By my reckoning, there have been at least twelve thousand five hundred "Thoughts", so it must have been quite a project. Apparently, some have been lost but Christine admits that there were many that she would have liked to include. Just over one hundred and sixty made it into this three hundred-page book, each one very much worth a read.

The "Thoughts" are separated into eight chapters, each containing between fourteen and twenty-four contributions. Just the chapter headings show the rich diversity of the "thoughts"selected: National, International, Culture and Society; Sex, Race and Social Change; Religion and Society; People; Science, Nature and Covid; and, finally, Life, Death and Faith.

The contributors come from a range of faith traditions. It was Jewish Rabbi Lionel Blue who broke the Christian exclusivity of "Thought" in the 1970s, but over the years he has been followed by Sikhs, Muslims, Buddhists and many more. Subjects have broadened over the decades; from memory, I really can't recall any "Thought"about sex in the 1970s, but by the 2010s it became a regular topic. There was one subject which was strangely absent: those of us who were active during the miners' strike in the mid-1980s, noticed how little sympathetic coverage the miners were given by the BBC; sadly, this did extend into religious broadcasting, including "Thought".

At least three of the "Thoughts" themselves created news as well as reflecting it.

Methodism's Colin Morris, created controversy on St David's Day 1971, when "Thought" was still in its infancy. Morris ridiculed the government's racist immigration policy which divided us into "patrials"—someone with a parent born in the UK and therefore entitled to move here —and "non-patrials": basically everyone else and, therefore, with no right to be here. He pointed out that St David, St George and St Andrew would have qualified as "non-patrials", as they weren't born in the UK. He slipped in that wonderful quote of Paul found in Galatians 3:28 and finished by asking the government to think again because the policy was alien to the spirit of the greatest "non-patrial" of all: Jesus of Nazareth. Cue controversy and Colin was dropped for a while.

"Bishop Jim", as we called the then Bishop of Stepney Jim Thompson, probably destroyed his preferment to Birmingham in 1984 when he suggested politicians should give up politics for Lent. It was during the controversy over the Church of England report "Faith in the City". The Tory government told the church to stay out of politics. Bishop Jim's retort was that to split God's world into spiritual and political would ghettoise religion and de-moralise politics.

Anne Atkins hit the headlines in 1996 with a stalwart defence of what was then seen to be the Christian view of homosexuality. It led to complaints and a great deal of anger. Just a few weeks later, she was offered a column in the Daily Telegraph. Had such a "Thought" been aired in the age of social media, there would no doubt have been death threats and visits to her home. But she made her point and made others think.

Many other talks reflected the news of the day: euthanasia, knife crime, the Rushdie affair, Princess Diana's death, the overturn of Roe v Wade, Ukraine, and Je suis Charlie are just some of the subjects of hastily written "thoughts" which tried to make sense in a world where there seemed, at times, to be no sense.

One of the most moving "thoughts" came from Canon Dr Giles Fraser as he reflected on the death of a police officer in France who had volunteered to be an exchange for a hostage in a French supermarket. Lieutenant

Colonel Beltrame went into the supermarket knowing there was a high probability he would be killed. He was described as a martyr, which is a witness to his faith. It was revealed that Beltrame came from a secular background but had found faith a few years before. It was said that he did not hide his faith, he radiated it. Fraser reminded us that Beltrame would have been inspired by the original and archetypal martyrdom of Christianity—the crucifixion of Christ.

Methodist Recorder 21st October, 2022

The Surprises and Challenges
of Black history

Did you know that the first Black rugby player capped for England made his international debut in 1909? Or that in 1700 there were twenty thousand Black people living in London? Just some of the things not many people know, be they Black or white, uncovered in the panel show **"Sorry, I Didn't Know"** (ITV) which ran during October, Black history month.

Jimmy Peters was the rugby player and he certainly had a colourful life. Sadly, a touring South African team objected to his inclusion in the England side and he was dropped, eventually making his way to rugby league. It wasn't until 1988 that England fielded another Black rugby union international.

Perhaps we could be forgiven for forgetting an early 20th century rugby player, but **"Whoever Heard of a Black Artist? Britain's Hidden Art History"** (BBC4) brought us to more recent times. Post-war Britain saw the first arrival of large communities of Black and Asian people, and with them came their artists such as Althea McNish, Aubrey Williams and Frank Bowling. At first, they were welcomed, even celebrated, by the art establishment with a sense of optimism. Then the racism and exclusiveness in the art world kicked in. Their works were collected, with at least two thousand in thirty major public collections, but now rarely displayed. There are plans for a major exhibition in Manchester to bring these works back into public view, but it is sad that such distinguished people are marginalised and forgotten.

Since listening to **"Swimming Against the Tide"** (Radio 4) my mind keeps going back to those wonderful few days when the £72 million Sandwell Aquatic Centre became the venue for this year's Commonwealth Games swimming and diving competitions. Sandwell is one of the most diverse communities in the UK, yet as we gave out Bibles to the arriving spectators, very few of them were Black or Asian. We spent a morning ourselves as spectators and noticed that none of the competitors, from any Commonwealth country, were Black.

Now in her forties, mother Joyce Osei also noticed that, when she took her children to swimming lessons, very few of the other learners were Black, like hers. Sport England has now found that 95 per cent of Black adults and 80 per cent of Black children don't swim. Astonishingly, there is apparently a myth that Black people have heavier bones which makes it more difficult to float. Swimming is a wonderful way of exercising and we need to encourage young people of all communities to enjoy its benefits.

The first Black woman I remember meeting was the midwife who attended the birth of my sister when I was just three years old. Since then, I've met Black women as friends, as churchgoers and as a line manager. **"Judi Love: Black, Female and Invisible"** (Channel 4) confronts each of us, especially men, with the prospect that we may be "misogynoir", having a dislike, distrust and prejudice against Black women. The place of Black women in our society is traced through childhood, into motherhood, the workplace and business. Having a black skin and being female brings a double judgment and assumptions, which are often unsaid but have a catastrophic impact on self-esteem. We are used to thinking of our Black population being concentrated in our cities but even in country towns there are Black families. This programme is a must-see for anyone meeting with these families, especially teachers, clergy, and healthcare professionals.

The return of **"The Larkins"** (ITV1) will give us something to cheer ourselves up after Sunday evening services between now and Christmas. There are new arrivals in this series who will keep our attention. The new neighbours, the Jerebohms, clearly "Nouveau", could lead to a war of attrition. Early on, it seems that Ma and Pop Larkin are getting the upper hand. But the stationing of the handsome Anglican, The Rev Candy, has set young female hearts fluttering.

"Opera on 3: Vaughan William's The Pilgrim's Progress" (Radio 3) is well worth a catch-up on BBC Sounds, but sadly only for another fortnight. This recording was made in 2012 and is presented by Andrew McGregor in conversation with Oliver Soden, who gives some detailed background to the work, both the music and Bunyon's original book.

Our midweek viewing will certainly be the poorer as we see the final episodes of two much-loved drama programmes. The second series of the remake of **"All Creatures Great and Small"** (Channel5) has once again been a joy as we see the vet's practice noticing the clouds of war on the horizon. James seems more settled in the community but is wondering whether he should "join up", despite being newly married. Tristan, rather typically, seems to go his own sweet way. Siegfried appears to be getting more reliant on housekeeper Mrs Hall. Let's hope there's another series; wartime veterinary services may present more challenges.

It's also farewell to **"Doc Martin"** (ITV1) with his return to London. I'm not certain how his wife Louisa will fare in the big city, or how the Doc himself will manage without the support and counsel of Mrs Tishall and PC Penhale. Alas we will never know as, after seventy-eight episodes, this is the last series. My Cornish-heritage wife loves it, but can't explain why it never rains in Port Wenn and none of the locals begin every conversation with the weather. Not like the Cornwall we visit!

Methodist Recorder 28th October, 2022

We Have More Choice, but after 100 years the BBC reigns supreme

When the BBC celebrated its 50th anniversary in 1972, there were just three national TV channels, two of which were run by the BBC and four national BBC wireless services. BBC local radio was very much in its infancy and confined to urban areas.

How different the world of broadcasting is as the BBC marks its centenary: at least fifty free-to-air channels plus thirty-five satellite and cable channels. There are also multiple streaming services, thousands of podcasts and YouTube channels and each one of us can send moving and speaking messages around the world in an instant. As we found out during the Covid lockdown, even the smallest church can run a weekly broadcast.

Between 1922, and well into the 1950s, the BBC was very much on its own in the UK, albeit with competition from Radio Luxembourg and propaganda services such as Radio Moscow and the wartime Germany Calling. Yet, despite this recent competition, the BBC continues to dominate much of our viewing and listening. It created the ethos for public service broadcasting which is consciously observed, or ignored, around the world. The BBC's history is worth understanding.

"How the BBC Began" (BBC2) takes us back to the very early days of broadcasting when fledgling radio services were eventually handed over to the paternal care of John Reith, the son of a Scottish Presbyterian minister. There was no template and Reith's team had to start many programme and service ideas from scratch. A lovely interview from former Prime Minister Edward Heath revealed the excitement that he and many other children in the 1920s and 1930s had experienced as they heard live voices and music broadcast into their living rooms for the first time.

The BBC didn't always get it right. The rolling news format had yet to be invented but that is exactly what happened on the fateful evening in 1963 when President Kennedy was shot. Confusion and chaos reigned behind the scenes but for those of us in the bar of the Bermondsey Territorial Army Drill Hall, the news and comment filtered through as we absorbed the news. No one who saw it will ever forget the edition of the satirical programme "That Was The Week That Was" the following evening.

BBC TV brought us some special moments to mark its centenary: King Charles appeared on **"The Repair Shop"** (BBC1) the contestants of **"Strictly Come Dancing"** (BBC1) had to make the best of various BBC programme theme tunes, and BBC4 devoted an entire week's evening programming to replaying over fifty situation comedies from the last forty years.

It was BBC radio which devoted some serious time to reflect on the role of the BBC, especially in those critical first decades of its existence. **"Archive on 4: The Battle of the Brows"** (Radio 1) detailed the very real strains and stresses within the BBC during the 1930s as they tried to live up to John Reith's mantra that their role was to "inform, educate and entertain". The concept of people of intelligence and education as having "high brows" and the rest of us, was part of the cod science of phrenology which emerged in the nineteenth century. Some in the BBC believed that opening the sounds of the concert hall and theatre to all would enable millions more to enjoy the finer arts. Others were convinced that there needed to be programmes which were aimed at different audiences. This led to the creation of two services which opened shortly before the war: The Home Service and The Light Programme. The Third Programme was started within fourteen months of the cessation of hostilities and was seen as a force for good by focusing on the arts. During my time in BBC local radio, I was very conscious that our training and the station management were constantly trying to keep a delicate balance between popular culture and serious local issues.

"Sunday Worship" (Radio 4) is commemorating the BBC centenary with a visit to the highest peaks in the UK. Radzi Chinyanganya and Rev Grace Thomas started with Scafell Pike. Admittedly, I was driving on the motorway with a very heavy storm raging around me, so I may not have been paying enough attention, but it left me feeling "is that it?". They talked about the benefit of praying on a mountainside, always a special blessing, and then talked about "hope" without mentioning Jesus. In fact, the only time Jesus was mentioned, as far as I can remember, was a reference to "our Saviour" to introduce the Lord's Prayer and another reference to "the Son" in the blessing. My fears were confirmed when they played out to William Blake's mystic and speculative "Jerusalem"; great song, but not a Christian hymn.

James Bond, aka the actor Daniel Craig, and I have our shoes handmade at Crockett and Jones in Northampton. It isn't cheap, but the shoes last much longer than the imported stuff on the high street. **"The 007 Shoe Factory: We Are England"** (BBC1) went behind the scenes and showed us the skill and patience that went into every pair. It was especially encouraging to know that they regularly employ apprentices who they train to keep this British industry alive. There used to be two hundred and fifty firms of shoemakers in Northampton, now there are just seven firms left. It was good to see such a happy workforce.

Methodist Recorder 11th November, 2022

Behind the Scenes
at 'Strictly' with a former Home Secretary

Let's go behind the scenes of Britain's most popular TV series, with my old friend Jacqui Smith. She caused quite a stir when she appeared on **"Strictly Come Dancing"** (BBC1). It's not the sort of thing a former Home Secretary does!

Firstly, how on earth did she get to do "Strictly"? "I was very excited to be contacted in the spring of 2020 by the 'Strictly' team who said that I was in the frame," she explained. "They emphasised the positive nature of 'Strictly'. The feel was very much about learning something new and being celebrated for it, not being ridiculed as in some reality shows. I was in my late fifties and felt that this would be a brilliant adventure. I hadn't danced since I was about six so I knew it would be a real challenge.

"When they finally decided in the July of that year, I had to keep it secret until the announcement—this was one of the most difficult bits!".

Jacqui is full of praise for her professional partner, Anton Du Beke, who "was really lovely and, of course, I was his last partner as, after me, he became a judge".

"I like to think that he couldn't top dancing with me! He is a really good teacher and we rehearsed in various different studios near to where I was living in London. Because it was Covid year, I had to move away from home into a flat for six weeks on my own so I could be in a bubble with Anton. It was hard work, with practice for about six or seven hours each day and filming for the other bits included in that.

"Anton was good at making me a cup of tea and giving me a biscuit when I was flagging and we had some great chats—he is really interested in politics and had previously partnered Anne Widdecombe."

Jacqui assured me that the Saturday night show "is absolutely live which is the most terrifying, and exciting, part about it." The results show on Sunday is apparently pre-recorded, but Jacqui wouldn't say anymore!

Judge Craig Revel Horwood often comes in for criticism because of his sparky comments to some contestants. Jacqui found just how unpleasant that can be: "Craig was really mean to me but I get that he's like a pantomime villain and I didn't take it too personally. There were only three judges in my year as Bruno couldn't come from the US but Shirley Ballas and Motsi Mabuse were really encouraging."

The moment every contestant dreads is being chosen for the "dance off". Jacqui was the first to go in her year, how did that feel? "I was sad, but not too surprised to be in the dance off on my first week. Anton thought we would escape, but there were fewer people than usual as it was Covid time and a high standard from the start. I had already decided that I would completely throw myself into it and I'm proud to say that I did. There aren't many people who can say that they have danced live on TV and been lifted into the air on a trapeze with feather fans all around!"

But after Craig's criticism and the stress of the dance off, did she enjoy it, and would she do it again? "I loved it. It really was the adventure I hoped it would be and whilst I would love to do it again, it really is a once in a lifetime experience." Well done Jacqui, it took a lot of guts.

"Exit Game" (Radio 4) is all about those very young men and boys who dedicate their lives to football. For some, it leads to riches beyond comprehension; to others, absolute heartbreak. This drama documentary sheds light on the highly competitive academy youth system employed by British clubs to claim and develop their talent. It's based on some careful research, which makes it all the more disturbing. Readers involved with youth work or secondary education may like to catch up on BBC Sounds.

I intended to watch, but not review **"Wendy Craig: All the Laughs and More"** (Channel 5). I knew she had appeared in a "situation comedy" in the 1970s called "Butterflies". Wendy plays Rhia, an unappreciated mother and wife in a loveless marriage who has fantasies about an affair. Apparently, Wendy had mailbags of letters from women telling her that she was portraying their marriages. It felt sad.

In **"Life Changing: Ripple Effect"** (Radio 4) Erica Rhodes was in a crowded street when a man collapsed in front of her. She took the split-second decision to save his life with newly acquired first aid skills. She gave her address to the man's colleague, for him to return a handkerchief. An angry wife, a divorce, a civil partnership, a wedding and friendships that lasted for the next twenty or thirty years followed.

Sometimes it's worth searching around on Freeview to find the real gems. After years of being on subscription TV, **"Modern Family"** (E4) is now free to air. It's an American sitcom about three interrelated families in Los Angeles. This 'mockumentary' aims to portray the perils and joys of family life. Each thirty-minute episode is a story within itself, but there is an overriding narrative that this new viewer will eventually find. Unlike many American comedies, it is actually funny.

Methodist Recorder 18th November, 2022

Ram Gidoomal
– the refugee who came to know Jesus

Ram Gidoomal is from that remarkable wave of refugees of Asian origin who sought sanctuary in the United Kingdom, following harassment and deportation from their adopted homes in East Africa. He tells his moving, remarkable, and at times shocking story in **"My Silk Road The Adventures and Struggles of a British Asian Refugee"** (Pippa Rann) a book that should be on the bookshelf of anyone wanting to know more about the Indian community in Britain.

Ram's family had already fled from India following the partition of 1947. They had moved to Mombasa, in Kenya, where his father established a very successful business importing luxury silks from China and Japan. He had enjoyed his schooldays with other children from the South Asian diaspora. Though from the very different faiths, Hinduism and Islam, all got on well. Ram's family were Hindus.

It all changed one evening when he was seventeen. Ram's father came home very distressed: the Kenyan government had served a deportation order on him. Then came another shock: the message from India was clear, "You chose to be British, let the Queen look after you." With stringent currency restrictions, the family began the painful move to London where they ran a corner shop. His father did not take the move well, because having been uprooted twice, he feared that it might happen a third time.

Ram also found the shock of a new culture and a different climate hard. His father taught him everything he could about business, especially the arrangements made to raise the capital from family and friends to launch a business. Shortly after his father returned to Kenya to wrap up his affairs, he suffered a stroke and died. Ram had to adapt very quickly and created a lifetime's maxim: "Never let what you can't do stop you from doing what you can." The family businesses flourished and, soon, Ram felt able to call London his home.

Then there was the first of several unexpected events which were to change his life. We have all seen those leaflets from groups such as the Scripture Gift Mission; we may have even given them out, wondering if these seeds would ever bear fruit. Sometime in Mombasa, his family had been given a booklet called "Daily Strength". Ram was enthralled by it, unaware that it was Christian scripture, but so impressed he learnt some parts by heart.

One evening he was in a pub and began speaking to some musicians about a man from Galilee. Over several weeks, he began to read the Bible. There was a lot of confusion and a lot of questions, but one evening he decided to open the door to Jesus. From that moment, his prayers changed and he felt he truly had a personal faith. As I read Ram's account, I wondered why this newspaper isn't full of similar accounts as people discover the wonderful gifts of God.

His business prospered and Ram became a very rich man with contacts throughout the world. He married the woman he loved and they started a family. He settled into his Christian faith. He clearly adores his Indian heritage and sees no conflict with his new faith. But there was a restlessness about how he could express his Christian commitment.

One day whilst visiting Mumbai, having signed a number of very profitable deals, his life was to change yet again. A representative of the International Fellowship of Evangelical Students took him to the shanty town of Dharavi. Ram knew it would be bad, but it was far worse than anything he had imagined. He saw a small boy, about five years old, the same age as his son, but he wore rags, was dirty and thin. At first he was told the boy lived in a cardboard box, but that was corrected: the child lived in a stinking pipe. Ram asked where his parents were and his guide pointed to some cages where girls, some only on the cusp of puberty were imprisoned, awaiting their next abuser.

Ram would never unsee that child or his imprisoned mother and began to ask questions about how his Christianity was compatible with his wealth, whilst young people lived in such squalor, poverty and powerless. He soon teamed up with Oasis founder Steve Chalke and began to use his contacts, skills, enthusiasm and wealth to generate millions of pounds to support people in poverty.

This autobiography reminds us that lives can be changed, that Jesus is still calling people from other faiths and traditions to the foot of the cross, and that each one of us can make a positive difference for others. It also reminds us that those refugees, who are so despised by some, bring fresh insights which can enhance us all.

Methodist Recorder 18th November, 2022

TV Cooking Competitions
in the age of the foodbank

It is still possible to watch Fanny Cradock—TV cook of the 1960s and 70s—give well-meant and concise cooking instructions on You Tube. Her focus is on the job in hand and by the end of each programme the viewer has enough information to cook for themselves. Ideal for struggling parents.

Cookery programmes are now buried on daytime television, except as yet another "reality" competition. Last week, a quirk of the scheduling meant that the two flagship cookery competitions, complete with barking judges, timed projects and the oh-so-familiar heart-stopping results sequence, overlapped by fifteen minutes.

The cookery competitions were in a different world to the previous evening's **"Panorama: Why is food so expensive?"** (BBC1). We heard parents describe how they are trying to stretch their income to feed their families. The story from a food bank in Liverpool is shocking, but many Methodists will already be well aware that families in our congregations and the wider community are struggling.

The Panorama team outlined many of the factors which are driving up prices, but then revealed that prices on specific items vary in different shops within the same chain. It was very discouraging with predictions that prices are set to rise even higher. This may be the time for television to produce programmes which help families make the best use of food on a diminishing budget. We certainly need more information about rising prices and how to beat them.

Meanwhile on **"The Great British Bake Off: the Final"** (Channel 4) we saw something of the diversity of talent we now have in the country's kitchens. All four finalists were from our ethnic minorities and were able to bring some extra ingredients to the table. Various amateur cooks had been whittled down to the final three with Sandro, Syabira and Abdul battling it out with three carefully chosen cooking projects. On the whole, the competition seemed relaxed, though we were always aware of the time pressure. The summer pudding bombe turned out to be a mess, but Syabira's final "edible sculpture" was a real showstopper and a deserved winner.

"MasterChef: the Professionals" (BBC1) saw four young chefs, again from our minority communities, battle it out for a place in the quarter finals. The first project saw the contestants butchering a rack of pork, big enough to feed a family for a couple of days, and then serve up a chop. Unlike **"Bake Off"**, the judges took time to explain the techniques and gave us some tips for the future.

There was one contestant who reminded us that families do struggle to provide food on the table. Each contestant was asked to produce a "signature dish". A young woman from Albania provided a meal created from just one ingredient: the turnip. The judges admired her skills but found it amusing that someone could find eight different ways to cook a turnip, they didn't understand. Extreme poverty means cooks have to be creative, just as our forebears were when they created the Yorkshire pudding.

I remember chatting to former President of Conference, Donald Soper, in the late sixties. Kingsway Hall, where he was Minister, backed onto Covent Garden. He mentioned how the wives of the porters at the market would take the vegetables that were unsold because they were "tired" and turned them into healthy feasts, so despite their poverty, the families ate well. Historian David Olusoga told us more in **"The People's Piazza: a History of Covent Garden"** (BBC2).

Originally the former garden of a convent close to London was laid out by the Earl of Bedford as an Italian-style piazza for the very rich. Civil war and plague soon followed and the character of Covent Garden changed, with coffee houses and brothels coming to dominate the area. People also found it a useful space in which to sell fruit, vegetables and flowers. Within a few decades, it became the centre of country's food distribution network for fruit and vegetables, as well as feeding London.

Do the British have **"A Fish Phobia"** (Radio 4)? If you missed it, try to catch-up on BBC Sounds. Angela Hartnett visited Brixham in Devon and was amazed at the wide variety and quantity of fish landed. However more than 80 per cent of it will be exported and the nearest it will get to British stomachs is those of tourists in France, Italy and Spain. Whiting, John Dory, Dover Sole and cuttlefish go abroad. Meanwhile 80 per cent of the fish we eat, mainly cod, is imported—some even from China. Our seas are teeming with herring and mackerel but very little is fished and rarely served. We are advised to pop down to our fishmonger and try out new species. Try finding a fishmonger on a British high street - ours closed down in 1975.

The message is clear: the British ought to be more adventurous about the fish we eat. Too many of us reject fish and seafood that we haven't even tried. We need to be far more open minded.

"Food Unwrapped: Store Cupboard Staples" (Channel 4) took us behind the scenes at the factory where they produce Marmite. They take the waste yeast from the beer industry's brewing process, add some secret ingredients and turn out a tasty product that my son absolutely loves. Some people love it, others hate it. Personally, I can't stand the stuff, I've never even tried it, and probably won't.

Methodist Recorder 25th November, 2022

After Such an Horrific History,
Jews don't count

East London in the 1950s had one of the biggest concentrations of Jewish people in the world. I was born just two doors down from a Hebrew school. Nearly half of my school mates were Jews. I noticed that several of their mothers had numbers tattooed on their arms.

I also remember meeting people who assured me they cared deeply for animal welfare, so called for a boycott of Jewish shops by deliberately misrepresenting Kosher slaughter. Sixty years later, I attended a Methodist meeting. There was a report by an anonymous "theology group" which urged Christians to "boycott all goods on sale in supermarkets and shops which support the state of Israel". How do we know what a shopkeeper thinks about Israel? Ah yes, of course. Then it was Kosher slaughter; now it's Israel. These people haven't gone away; they will always find a reason for anti-Semitism, and they will package it to be acceptable to the well-meaning.

The comedian David Baddiel did a remarkable job in deconstructing the idea that growing tolerance to minority groups will inevitably help protect Jews from anti-Semitism. **"Jews Don't Count"** (Channel 4) gave several well-known Jews the opportunity to tell us about the discrimination they had experienced. Sometimes, it was conscious, at other times so deeply embedded that the perpetrators didn't understand why what they said and did was so offensive.

Baddiel himself has come to recognise that his black-face portrayal of Black footballer Jason Lee in the 1990s comedy programme "Fantasy Football" was offensive and racist. On air, he offered a fulsome face-to-face apology to Jason. It didn't make for comfortable viewing but was clearly well overdue.

In case we think Methodism is free from such discrimination, we should ponder the names of three Jewish women: Marianne Grunfeld, Therese Steiner and Auguste Spitz. In fact, this is probably the first time their names have been mentioned in any publication connected to Methodism. Since 1995, thanks to research by the writer Madeleine Bunting, we have known that a Methodist Minister was involved in their deportation from Guernsey to the Nazi death camps. Despite making prime-time news bulletins when the link was exposed, and my letter to the President of Conference, there has been absolutely no apology or acknowledgement that a Methodist was involved in this crime. David Baddiel has had the guts to apologise. But for Methodism, these three Jewish women don't count. This programme will make uncomfortable viewing for some, but please make time to catch-up on All 4.

"Bad Blood: The Story of Eugenics" (Radio 4) tells us just how dangerous well-meaning ideas can be. Eugenics was a word invented by Francis Galton, born about a quarter of a mile from our home, to describe his scientific ideas to "improve" the human race by selective breeding. He believed genes determined life's outcome. In Victorian Britain, he believed he had plenty of evidence. Some families did very well; others lived in squalor. Their state was nothing to do with social, educational or economic conditions. Galton even invented the phrase "nature vs nurture". He called for a "jihad", or a holy war, to improve the national stock. Britain's wealthy and well-to-do loved the idea and a whole movement grew up around eugenics. In Northern Europe, these ideas were enthusiastically adopted because blonde blue-eyed people were seen to be superior to other racial groups.

There was a dark side. Those who were seen to have good genes had to be careful that they didn't contaminate their blood line by reproducing with those from inferior stock. Whilst the good looking and the wealthy could choose the ideal breeding partner, there were suggestions that the less blessed should be prevented from having children and thereby eliminated. Across the world these theories were used to enforce sterilisation of disabled people and eventually used to justify the extermination of Jews.

Right up until the weekend before Christmas, our television schedules will be dominated by **"The World Cup"** (BBC1 and ITV1). Obviously, a weekly review cannot do justice to this controversial tournament. I want to take my hat off to the Iranian players, who we saw standing in silence during their national anthem as a sign of solidarity with women in their country who won't accept the strict rules about headdress. That protest took guts. These footballers will pay a price.

If you can't stand football still take time to catch-up with **"Green Lions: Cameroon '90"** (BBC4). It's the fairytale story of how impoverished Cameroon took on the World Cup holders, Argentina, in the opening game of the 1990 competition. There's something for everyone, especially those who are interested in international development, sport, Africa and a really good true-life story.

I watched **"Naughty Tories: John Major and Edwina Currie"** (Channel 5) mainly because I had been Edwina's press officer when she was Chair of Birmingham Social Services Committee in 1980. She was quite impressive and, on occasions, personable. My wife wanted me to switch the programme off because it was so nasty, prurient and offensive. A full fifth, possibly a quarter, of the programme featured various wannabes and has-beens sniggering about what happened between a couple in their thirties way back in 1984. These things are a matter for the people concerned, their spouses, and no one else. Edwina was mistaken to "kiss and tell" twenty years ago, but both she and John Major, whatever their politics, deserve better.

Methodist Recorder 2nd December, 2022

History Is Never About the Past,
and what about those Christmas ads?

The debut of **"Simon Schama's History of Now"** (BBC2) came less than twelve hours before London's Wellcome Museum announced it was closing the "Medicine Man" gallery because it told "a global story in which disabled people, Black people, indigenous peoples and people of colour were exoticised, marginalised and exploited—or even missed out altogether". Naturally, there was predictable anger from some sections of the press at the idea that this gallery, first created in the early 2000s, represented a history of the UK which we cannot now possibly question.

Schama takes a personal view of the history that he himself has lived through. He shows how being unable to question and revise history can take us to some dangerous places. This is far from dusty archives or curated objects: modern tyrannies try to falsify the past for their own ends, and, in so doing, are able to falsify both the present and the future.

He identifies one hope when people find themselves in dark places: the ability of artists, writers and performers to create a counter narrative, resistance and reaction. Unexpectedly, we find ourselves confronted with Pussy Riot's outrageous performance art in a Moscow Cathedral and our response is sympathy rather than disgust. Schama shows how this demonstration in Moscow fits directly with the oppression and imprisonment of dissidents in Czechoslovakia fifty years before. He reminds us just how precious our democracy is, but like many precious things, often fragile, as Donald Trump so ineloquently demonstrates.

At this time of the year we turn to our Bibles to remember the story of our Lord's nativity. Priest and theologian, John Barton, asked a simple question on **"Start the Week, Faith Lost in Translation"** (Radio 4): what did the wise men say to the shepherds? Well, we don't know if they even met, despite our time-honoured Sunday school nativity tableaux. The wise men are in the Gospel of Matthew but not in Luke, whereas the shepherds are in Luke but not in Matthew. Barton wasn't being a clever-clogs liberal—he was merely explaining how our scriptures came to be written, and subsequently translated, from different perspectives.

Barton was talking about his recent book "The Word: On the translation of the Bible" which describes how the Bible has been translated into thousands of versions across seven hundred languages. He explained the difference between an "original" and a "functional" translation. For him, the importance of any translation was that it is the repository of a sacred story. Listen on BBC Sounds or put his book on your Christmas wish-list.

For eighteen years, Richard Gamble has followed his vision of building a "Wall of Answered Prayer" in the West Midlands. **"The Untold: The Prayer Wall"** (Radio 4) tells the story of his interaction with God, how the Holy Spirit led him and others to make it happen, and why one day as we travel along the M42, M6 or on HS2, we will see a structure bigger than the "Angel of the North" proclaiming one million answered prayers. This will really irritate some readers, so all the more reason to listen on catch-up.

When I worked in advertising, we said "nothing works like television". In the next fortnight, our television sets will be working overtime to persuade us to spend our Christmas pounds with rival stores. This year's ads have certainly been a mixed bag, but will they succeed?

"Have Your Elf a Merry Christmas" (Asda) is a cheerful film but products and prices are noticeable by their absence. You may like to catch up on YouTube with a short film that tells you how the ad was made. There's lots of new technology, but it seems that it was made for the boardroom, rather than the customers.

Surprisingly the "discounters" have the most bizarre ads. **"Will Kevin be Home for Christmas?"** (Aldi) features a family of carrots on a trip to Paris. Somehow, a carrot becomes a snowman's... well, let's just say we know he is male. **"The Story of Lidl Bear"** (Lidl) stars a stiff, sour-faced teddy bear that becomes a media sensation whilst a little girl mourns his absence at home, but all is well Christmas morning. Is that it?

Two of the bigger supermarkets promote good causes. **"Gifts that Give"** (M&S) boasts that M&S donated £1 million of its £309 million profits to community causes, but tells us little else. In **"The Beginner"** (John Lewis and Partners) a middle-aged couple are excited as they prepare their home for Christmas. On Christmas Eve, a teenage girl arrives on their doorstep, evidently to share

Christmas with them. Action for Children collaborated with the project and hope it will help start a national conversation about children in care. It doesn't sell, but I doubt if it helps those young people.

Thank goodness for **"Farmer Christmas"** (Morrisons) and to a lesser extent **"Once Upon A Time"** (Sainsbury's). Both tell a story, with the farmer approving of Morrison's Christmas range and a medieval countess enjoying the latest high quality produce from Sainsbury. Comprehensible and happy.

My vote goes to **"The Christmas Party"** (Tesco). It's a dummy party political broadcast which picks up on the lack of joy about at the moment, but promises to do something about it. Tesco's promise to provide dinner for five at under £25 is easily understood. Great fun, great visuals and a bit of humour. Tesco understands its audience.

Methodist Recorder, 9th December, 2022

Gyles Brandreth
Elizabeth: An Intimate Portrait

In this day and age, it is easy to believe that few of us pray. It is comforting to know that our late Queen Elizabeth II made a point of repeating the Lord's Prayer on her knees by her bed, every day of her life. She was a committed Christian and believed in the power of prayer and the importance of forgiveness.

Throughout the 561 pages of Gyles Brandreth's wide ranging biography, **"Elizabeth: An Intimate Portrait"** (Michael Joseph) her simple, uncluttered faith shines through some very dark chapters in the life of her family and Commonwealth. In Elizabeth's very first Christmas broadcast in 1952, and looking forward to her Coronation, she asked her people to: "Pray for me, that God may give me wisdom and strength to carry out the solemn promises I shall be making, and that I may faithfully serve Him and you, all the days of my life."

It is interesting to note that Elizabeth agreed to meet the American evangelist Billy Graham at a time when many in the mainstream church rejected his theology of atonement, and discussed with him the power of the blood that was shed on the cross. Her marriage, sanctified by God, was the most important relationship of her life. When Philip died, at the height of the recent Covid pandemic, much was made of Elizabeth sitting alone at his funeral. But she did not feel alone. In church, she was with God and at difficult times it was, for her, the place to find comfort and consolation.

George Carey, a former Archbishop of Canterbury, said: " The Queen always weighs her words. If she says something or someone is in her prayers, she means it. She will be on her knees praying, exactly as she has promised."

Elizabeth's belief in redemption was evident in 1995 when she insisted that the disgraced Cabinet minister John Profumo sat next to her at a dinner to mark Margaret Thatcher's 70th birthday. Profumo had rocked the British establishment in the 1960s by having an affair with a "call girl". Since then, he had devoted himself to public service in the East End of London, and Elizabeth wanted to make her support for his redemption clear for all to see.

Elizabeth understood that her role was one of duty and service. She was often "on show" but was aware that she represented something very special to her people. She was "seen" and always dignified. She never swore or lost her temper in public. Both she and Philip were aware that the media would have loved to create a soap opera around them, something sadly her children and grandchildren have not appreciated.

Even during her childhood and adolescence, Elizabeth understood her future role by being sensible and sensitive to those around her. Once she was of age, as the Second World War was thankfully approaching its end, she was able to join with other young women, from all classes, on an ATS car mechanics course at Aldershot.

Brandreth had met both Elizabeth and Philip many years ago. He understood that senior royalty offer friendliness but not friendship. He worked with Philip when he was President of the National Playing Fields Association, and was eventually asked to write Philip's biography. This gave him an opportunity to undertake quite extensive research, both archival and oral. He also keeps a diary, quite detailed it seems, in which he recorded his discussions with, and about, the Royal Family. He makes absolutely no bones about his respect and belief in the concept of monarchy, and his admiration for the family destined to be our kings and queens.

The style of this book is very easy to read, more like a conversation and a little gossipy in the nicest sense. Brandeth reading extracts would make a wonderful "Book of the Week" for Radio 4 or a podcast. He traces Elizabeth's family back to the time of Queen Victoria. He draws many parallels with some of the challenges faced by the Queen and her family in recent years with those of her forebears. He confronts the most serious allegations against the late Queen's family, which gives his work an additional authenticity.

In the future, Gyles should consider writing a detailed account of Elizabeth's dealings with the Commonwealth. She, more than anyone else, helped the transition from Empire to a new and lasting relationship. The lack of detailed footnotes and an index will sadly mitigate against its value to future historians. However, it's a cracking good read and fills in many gaps that only come from proximity and careful recording.

Possibly the most moving chapter is that which records the sadness following the collapse of Charles and Diana's marriage. Elizabeth made it clear: that Diana was in her prayers. Our late Queen prayed, and her prayers will be missed.

Methodist Recorder, 16th December, 2022

DAVID J A HALLAM

'There's Not Much on the Telly,
let's see what's on the wireless'

Our hearts would sink when Dad decided that the "wireless" might provide better entertainment than what the two black-and-white channels were offering in the 1950s. These last few weeks, I'm beginning, more than sixty years later, to understand what he meant.

Football's **World Cup 2022** (ITV1) and **World Cup Match of the Day Live** (BBC1) have driven a steamroller through the late autumn schedules for prime-time TV. Even Channel 4 has delved into the film archives rather than risk pitting new material against the football leviathan.

On just one Saturday evening, apart from the football, we were offered old films such as Pretty Woman, Downton Abbey, Spiderman, Titanic and The Spy Who Dumped Me. It seems paralysis has set in. Thank goodness it's all over tomorrow evening, with, hopefully, the schedulers looking to put these big fixtures on BBC3 and ITV3 in future, which is surely what these channels should be for?

There were some bright spots: for example, **"Cadbury at Christmas"** (Channel 5) delved behind the scenes at the Bourneville factory and bought us some Christmas cheer without questioning the sourcing of the cocoa, as a previous programme had done just before Easter.

Our wonderful BBC Radio stepped in to provide some alternatives. **"Faith in Music"** (Radio 4) is getting a welcome second outing and is also available on BBC Sounds. Sir James MacMillan looks at the lives of some of our greatest composers and finds that much of their work is reflective of the religious and philosophical backgrounds in which they grew up. Richard Wagner, for example, had a Lutheran upbringing, but in later life took an interest in Buddhism. He was anti-Semitic but had very close Jewish friends. Much of his work reflected a belief in redemption and during the turbulent year of revolution in 1848, he took his place on the barricades. MacMillan looks at other composers, including Leonard Bernstein, Amadeus Mozart, Gustav Mahler, and our own Edward Elgar and Ralph Vaughan Williams.

In **"Britain's Communist Thread"** (Radio 4) historian Camilla Schofield looks at how British working class people created the Communist Party of Great Britain in the early 1920s. Far from communism being an alien import, though often portrayed as such, it was the lives of people in pit villages such an Maerdy, in the Rhondda Valley, whose experiences brought together a philosophy of community and solidarity which easily fused with the ideals of Marxism. Following the 1917 Bolshevik revolution, British communists looked to Moscow and the new Soviet state for their inspiration. They believed the struggle in Spain was the crucible in which fascism, often seen as capitalism with the gloves off, would be defeated. Many young men joined the republican International Brigade and gave their lives in the Spanish Civil War. Others gradually learnt the full horror of "the terror" that enveloped the various communist factions, which thought it acceptable to execute one another. This is a disturbing story as it pits sincere idealism against brutal reality. One interesting observation: nowhere in the description of Maerdy was there any reference to religion or the chapel, which we are trained to believe was so influential at that time in South Wales.

Last week's **"Book of the Week: Night Terrors"** (Radio 4) saw writer Alice Vernon investigate the phenomenon of sleep, and the dreams and insomnia which accompany it. In scripture, we are told that old men shall dream dreams, that messages were delivered by dreams. The cupbearer and the baker learnt of their fate by telling their dreams to Joseph. So, perhaps, we should learn more. Alice Vernon gives us an interesting introduction, so this is another worthwhile catch up.

Reader Martin Harker kindly contacted our editor and pointed out that **"Roger Bolton's Beeb Watch"** (Good Egg Productions) carries a fascinating episode in response to the claim that there has been a five-and-a-half million fall in the number of people in the UK describing themselves as Christian. The former head of BBC religious broadcasting, Ernie Rae, joins former "Feedback" presenter Roger Bolton in exploring the place of religion in the BBC's output. It is fairly clear that both have some issues about individuals at the BBC but their main arguments are worth considering. Whereas BBC Radio has a head of religion, BBC TV does not. That means there is no one championing the importance of the many faiths to which 82 per cent of the world's population claim some allegiance. Just as important, many of those working in broadcasting have little understanding, or even basic knowledge, of religions, and this leads to news output and scheduling which ignores any connection with faith. As a TV and radio reviewer for a denominational publication, I like to include at least one programme which is important to faith each week. This is comparatively easy for radio but I always struggle with TV —there is a limit to the number of reviews that can be written about "Songs of Praise"! This podcast is well worth a listen. If you are not used to finding podcasts just Google "Roger Bolton Podcast" on your device.

Finally, if, like Martin, you spot a programme or podcast which you think other readers would find useful, please feel free to contact us. With hundreds of podcasts and a growing number of TV channels and radio feeds, there is always something we miss! Our only request is that it should be accessible to all without subscription.

Methodist Recorder, 16th December, 2022

Harry Taylor
Victor Grayson: In search of Britain's Lost Revolutionary

David Hallam's 'book of the year'!

With a brilliant evocation of the political and spiritual activities on the streets of working class Liverpool through to an unsolved mystery, Harry Taylor's **"Victor Grayson: In Search of Britain's Lost Revolutionary"** (Pluto Press) is a gripping and entertaining read.

Victor Grayson was a gifted working class man from Liverpool, who was born in 1881. But there were questions about his true parentage. Apparently, he was tongue tied, which, given his future life as a public speaker and fiery left-wing Member of Parliament, comes as a surprise.

Grayson grew up in a community where, every night, there would be street corner meetings called by political and religious organisations. Grayson originally bounced between a gospel hall and the Unitarians, but it was the Unitarians who wanted to put him through ministerial training. They realised he could move a crowd. But he dropped out. Eventually, he became the MP for Colne Valley following a sensational by-election. However, he lost his seat three years later.

After that, Grayson lost his way. His closet homosexuality, combined with heavy drinking and a difficult marriage led to a breakdown. War service on the Western Front seemed to foretell a return to politics, but one day in 1920, he left his home with two men and was never seen again. Taylor tries, with some new evidence, to piece together what happened to Grayson, but alas with no definite conclusion. So, we finish with a mystery. I have my own theory! Read it and you will have yours.

Methodist Recorder, 23rd December, 2022

The Wicked "Contract"
that is destroying our Royal Family

My hazy view of Prince Harry a few years back was that of a very mixed up young man, possibly a bit of a lout, for whom the trauma of losing his mother would leave lasting scars. All that changed one Boxing Day as we walked the Malvern Hills. My phone rang and the caller announced themselves as being from **"Today"** (Radio 4).

Their guest editor was interested in a cutting I had sent in from the "50 years ago" feature in the **Methodist Recorder.** It told the story of Britain's first Black head teacher who had been appointed in 1967 to a school near where I live. On hearing the news, outsiders came and daubed the school with racist slogans and swastikas.

"Who is the guest editor?" I asked. "Prince Harry," was the reply. So, at 7:30pm the following morning, thanks to Prince Harry, I told the world the hitherto forgotten story of Anthony O'Connor and the racism he faced as he simply got on with his job.

In this column, I prefer to review free-to-air programmes, which all can see. But this week, the newspapers have been full of **"Harry and Meghan"** (Netflix). Most of the coverage has been overwhelmingly hostile to the Duke and Duchess of Sussex, often with a hint of racism. The Royal Family, wisely, are publicly saying nothing, but there are plenty of anonymous "friends", "sources" and "royal courtiers" keen to attack the couple. Many of these attack lines have been picked up on social media, with the addition of absolutely vile abuse.

What the programme shows is a young couple trying to explain why they had taken the extraordinary decision to leave the "gilded cage" of the Royal Family. Harry reveals the bizarre "contract" between a very particular white-dominated national press and the Royal Family. The argument is that the family is paid from the public purse and in return much of their life is public property, of which the selected newspapers are the arbiters. Harry summed it up as "we pay, you pose" with every member of the family, no matter how young and vulnerable, expected to "play the game".

We saw this "contract" in all its gruesome detail at Princess Diana's funeral. Whatever was the family thinking when it made two bereaved children walk over a mile, in full public view, behind their mother's coffin? Neither their father nor grandfather, who marched with them, even held their hands or put their arms around them.

Rather naively, the Duchess did not understand the contract. The moment her relationship with Harry became public, every detail of her life, her family, friends and colleagues became fair game for the British press. One male actor was offered $75,000 to say that he had slept with her, but he refused. She found herself under siege from the paparazzi—freelance photographers whose income depends on getting intrusive photographs—and her father's phone was hacked days before her wedding.

During the Platinum Jubilee celebrations, many noticed that Prince George was on a podium with his father dressed in a collar, tie and jacket. He was the only nine-year-old in the land wearing a tie on that balmy June evening. It seems that Harry's older brother hasn't learnt from his own experience.

Peter Townsend, Diana Spencer, Meghan Markle and others came to rue the day they got entangled with the Royal Family and its "contract". The late Queen kept it together, but a few more scandals and fall outs could see the end of this chapter in our history. Our Royal Family is in office by the Act of the Settlement 1701, which, like any other Act of Parliament, can be repealed. Contrary to the reviews you might read elsewhere, this programme is well worth watching.

As I heard the first instalment of **"Book of the Week: A Heart That Works"** (Radio 4) the news came in that three children aged eight, ten and eleven had died after falling through ice at a nearby mill pond. It's a very stark reminder that for many families there will be an overwhelming sense of sadness this Christmas. Rob Delany tells the story of the life and death of his son, Henry. It really isn't easy listening but may give some comfort to those who are bereaved and those who support them. It's on BBC Sounds until early January.

Will it be Quality Street or Roses after lunch on Boxing Day? Or the newcomers: Celebrations or Heroes? These are the happy choices offered in **"The Secret World of Christmas Chocolate"** (Channel 4) as we prepared for the festive feast. We learnt about the products creation and how the marketing managers fought for their market share. And, yes, they do change each year, and tubs don't have as many sweets as they did when you were a nipper.

Murder mysteries are not everyone's cup of tea, but if one turns up under the Christmas tree for you this year, then catch-up **"Agatha Christie: Lucy Worsley on the Mystery Queen"** (BBC2). It profiles an extraordinary writer, as Christie turned out entirely original fiction three or four times every year. Apparently, she was always a little hostile to her work being turned into film, but relented late in life so that we can enjoy "Murder on the Orient Express", "Miss Marple" and "Poirot". Re-runs will give us something to enjoy during the Christmas break.

Methodist Recorder, 23rd December, 2022

THE YEAR THE QUEEN DIED

DAVID J A HALLAM

Index of Reviews

1978: Winter of Discontent (Channel 5)   146

A Fish Phobia (Radio 4)   176

A Place in the Sun (More 4)   112

Agatha Christie: Lucy Worsley on the Mystery Queen (BBC2)   198

All Creatures Great and Small (Channel 5)   160

All-You-Can-Eat Buffets: How Do They Really Do It? (Channel 5)   76

An Inclusive Methodist Church (Methodist Podcast)   52

Angela Kalwaites (BBC Radio Devon)   96

Ant and Dec's Saturday Night Takeaway (ITV1)   35

Archetypes (Spotify)   127

Archive on 4: Disgusted, Mary Whitehouse (BBC Radio 4)   43

Archive on 4: The Battle of the Brows (Radio 1)   162

Archive on 4: Ziggy Stardust at 50 (Radio 4)   93

Are You Being Served?: Secrets and Scandals (Channel 5)   85

Bad Blood: The Story of Eugenics (Radio 4)   178

Bangers and Cash (Yesterday)   72

Banned! The Mary Whitehouse Story (BBC 2)   61

Bargain Loving Brits by the Sea (Channel 5)   93

Being Bridget Jones (BBC 4)   65

Beyond Reasonable Doubt: Britain's Rape Crisis (BBC1)   56

Blackpool's Dance Fever (BBC1)   131

Book of the Week: A Heart That Works (Radio 4)   197

Book of the Week: Iconoclasm (Radio 4)   90

Book of the Week: Metaphysical Animals (Radio 4)   37

Book of the Week: Night Terrors (Radio 4)   191

Book of the Week: On Consolation (Radio 4)   30

Book of the Week: Takeaway - Stories from a Childhood behind the Counter (BBC 4FM)   115

Boy Erased (BBC3)   36

Britain's Communist Thread (Radio 4)   190

Britain's Strictest Headmistress (ITV1)   81

Britten's War Requiem: Staging a Masterpiece (BBC 4)   84

By the Grace of God (BBC4)   69

Cadbury at Christmas (Channel 5)   189

Cadbury Exposed (Channel 4)   59

Call the Midwife (BBC1)   20

Carry On films (ITV3).,   66

Celebrity Lingo (ITV1)   139

Choral Evensong (Radio 3)   111

Commonwealth Games (BBC1, BBC2, and BBC3)   113

Conversations with Friends (BBC 3)   78

Couples Therapy (BBC2)   48

Coventry Cathedral: Building for a New Britain (BBC 4)   84

D.I.Ray (ITV)   67

Dad's Army (BBC 2)   81

Daily Service (Radio 4)   25

Dangerous Borders: A Journey across India and Pakistan (BBC4)   118

Davina McCall: Sex, Mind and the Menopause (Channel 4)   68

Death by Conspiracy (Radio 4)   41

Death on Daytime (Channel 4)   47

Deliveroo: How Do They Really Do It? (Channel 5)   76

Diana (ITV1)   126

Diana's Decades (ITV3)   126

Disappearance of Shannon Matthews (Channel 5)   48

DNA Journey (ITV1)   64

Do you want to write a book? (www.bondfieldmarketing.co.uk)   34

Doc Martin (ITV1)   160

Drama: The Reckoning (Radio 4)   78

EastEnders (BBC 1)   62

Everything I Know About Love (BBC 1)   89

Exit Game (Radio 4)   167

Faith in Music (Radio 4)   190

Fake Psychic (Radio 4)   24

Falklands War: the Untold Story (Channel 4)   55

Fantastic Beasts: a Natural History (BBC1)   41

Farmer Christmas (Morrisons)   184

File on Four: Isobel's Story (Radio 4)   147

Flights of Fancy: Pigeons and the British (BBC4)   124

Food Unwrapped: Store Cupboard Staples (Channel 4)   176

Freedom: 50 Years of Pride (Channel 4)   100

Freeze: Skating on the Edge (BBC3)   27

From Paris to Rome with Bettany Hughes (Channel 5)   145

Gifts that Give (M&S)   183

Glastonbury: 50 years and Counting (BBC 2)   92

Good Grief with Reverend Richard Coles (Channel 4)   119

Great British Railway Journeys (BBC 4)   85

Great Indian Railway Journeys: Lucknow to Kolkata (BBC2)   118

Green Lions: Cameroon '90 (BBC 4)   179

Gyles Brandreth (Profile)   103

Gyles Brandreth - Elizabeth: An Intimate Portrait (Michael Joseph)   185

Happy Campers: the Caravan Park (Channel 5)   51

Harry and Meghan (Netflix)   195

Harry Taylor - Victor Grayson: In search of Britain's Lost Revolutionary (Pluto Press)   193

Have Your Elf a Merry Christmas (Asda)   183

Heather Burton's DifferentAnglezShow (Newstyle)   140

Heatwave: Summer of '76 (Channel 5)   91

Here We Go (BBC1)   74

How the BBC Began (BBC2)   161

How to with John Wilson (BBC 2)   139

How to Write a Mills and Boon (BBC4)   38

In Patagonia with Huw Edwards (BBC4)   41

India 1947: Partition in Colour (Channel 4)   117

Inheritors of Partition (Radio 4)   119

Inside the Ritz Hotel (ITV3)   52

Inside the Superbrands (Channel 4)   94

Inside the Superbrands: Guinness (Channel 4)   95

Investigating Diana: Death in Paris (Channel 4)   127

Jay Blades: No Place Like Home (Channel 5)   70

Jeremy Vine Show (Radio 2)   54

Jews Don't Count (Channel 4)   177

Judi Love: Black, Female and Invisible (Channel 4)   158

Julia Bradbury: Breast Cancer and Me (ITV1)   68

Just One Thing with Michael Mosley (Radio 4)   65

Kate and Koji (ITV3)   42

Kathryn Stanczyszyn (BBC WM)   82

Last Night of the Proms (BBC1)   140

Learning to Read at 51 (BBC1) — 20

Last of the Summer Wine: 30 Years of Laughs (Channel 5) — 44

Laura Crompton (BBC Radio Manchester) — 151

Les Dawson: 30 Funniest Moments (Channel 5) — 120

LGBT+ History Month 2022 (The Methodist Podcast) — 29

Life Changing: Ripple Effect (Radio 4) — 167

Living Proof (TBNUK) — 53

Long Lost Family (ITV1)· — 101

Long Lost Family: Shipped to Australia (ITV1) — 63

Loose Women (ITV1) — 66

Louis Theroux's Forbidden America (BBC2) — 32

Love Island (ITV2) — 87

Lucy Worsley: Elizabeth I's Battle for God's Music (BBC 4) — 110

M*A*S*H (Great TV) — 66

Marriage (BBC1) — 123

MasterChef: the Professionals (BBC1) — 174

Maxine (Channel 5) — 151

Modern Family (E4) — 168

MPs under Threat (Channel 4) — 80

Music Matters (Radio 3) — 151

My Family, Partition and Me: India 1947 (BBC4) — 118

My Life as a Rolling Stone (BBC2) — 99

My Silk Road The Adventures and Struggles of a British Asian Refugee (Pippa Rann) — 169

Naughty Tories: John Major and Edwina Currie (Channel 5) — 180

Nazarnin (Radio 4) — 33

Neighbours (Channel 5) — 109

Ninja Warrior UK: Race for Glory (ITV1) — 139

Not Going Out (BBC1)   58

Once Upon A Time (Sainsbury's)   184

One Voice (https://methodist-churches-northampton.org.uk/podcasts) 73

Opera on 3: Vaughan William's The Pilgrim's Progress (Radio 3)   159

Our Dementia Choir Sings Again with Vicky McClure (BBC 1)   150

Panorama: Why is food so expensive? (BBC1)   173

Peaky Blinders (BBC1)   40

Perry Mason (CBS Drama)   66

Pilgrimage (BBC2)   46

Political Thinking with Nick Robinson (Radio 4)   98

Queen Elizabeth II   185

Red Rose (BBC3)   123

Rick Stein's Cornwall (BBC1)   24

Ridley (ITV1)   130

Roger Bolton's Beeb Watch (Good Egg Productions)   191

Room 5 (Radio 4)   19

Roots and Roofs Podcast,   97

RuPaul's Drag Race: UK vs the World (BBC3)   28

Saturday Live (Radio 4)   57

Secrets of the London Underground (Yesterday)   82

Secrets of the Queen's Coronation (Channel 4)   83

Seven Days in Summer: Countdown to Partition (BBC4)   117

Should I Buy an Electric Car? (Channel 5)   71

Simon Schama's History of Now (BBC2)   181

Simply Raymond Blanc (ITV1)   24

Something Understood: This is my vigil (Radio 4)   115

Songs of Praise (BBC 1)   95

Sorry, I Didn't Know (ITV)   157

Start the Week, Faith Lost in Translation (Radio 4)   182

Steps of Freedom: the Story of Irish Dance (BBC 4)   50

Strictly Come Dancing (BBC 1)   137

Sunday Worship (Radio 4)   163

Swimming against the Tide (Radio 4)   158

Ten Years Younger in Ten Days (Channel 5)   149

The Absolutely Fabulous June Whitfield (Channel 5)   148

The Archbishop Interviews (Radio 4)   37

The Archers (Radio 4)   69

The Beginner (John Lewis and Partners)   183

The Brittas Empire (Forces TV)   66

The Capture (BBC 1)   130

The Christmas Party (Tesco)   184

The Cruise (Channel 5)   93

The Dark Side of Direct Sales (Radio 4 FM)   132

The Diana Interview: the Truth behind the Scandal (Channel 4)   126

The Extraordinary Life of April Ashley (Channel 4)   100

The Fall of the House of Maxwell (BBC 2)   60

The Fight for Saturday Night (BBC4)   116

The Food Programme Fried Chicken: a Story of Race and Identity (Radio 4)   123

The Good Karma Hospital (ITV 1)   20

The Great British Bake Off: the Final (Channel 4)   174

The Great Cookbook Challenge (C4)   23

The Jubilee Pudding: 70 Years in the Baking (BBC 1)   75

The Labour Files (Al Jazeera)   147

The Larkins (ITV1)   159

The Listening Project (Radio 4)   86

The Masked Dancer (ITV1)   138

The Motorway (Channel 5)   73

The Murder of Alex Rodda: Social Media Murders (ITV1)   122

The Newsreader (BBC2)   109

The 007 Shoe Factory: We Are England (BBC1)   164

The Open Box (Radio 4)   60

The People's Piazza: a History of Covent Garden (BBC 2)   175

The Queen: 70 Glorious Years (BBC1)   28

The Queen's Platinum Jubilee Celebration (ITV1)   77

The Real Peaky Blinders (BBC2)   45

The Repair Shop (BBC1)   162

The Responder (BBC1)   21

The Rolling Stones Live at the Fonda (BBC2)   99

The Rolling Stones: Totally Stripped (BBC2)   100

The Secret World of Christmas Chocolate (Channel 4)   197

The Story of Lidl Bear (Lidl)   183

The Suspect (ITV)   129

The Untold: The Prayer Wall (Radio 4)   182

The Voice UK (ITV1)   138

The Witch Hunt: Lucy Worsley Investigates (BBC 2)   79

The Witches Pardon (Radio 4)   49

The Witchfinder (BBC 2)   49

The World Cup (BBC1 and ITV1)   179

The World's Most Scenic Rivers (Channel 5)   25

This is Going to Hurt (BBC1)   31

Thought for the Day, fifty years of inspiring thoughts   153
and reflections (BBC Books)

Trigger Point (ITV 1)   21

Today (Radio 4)   195

Ukraine   39

Unreal: A Critical History of Reality TV (Radio 4)   88

What Really Happened in the 90s (Radio 4)   69

White Debt (Radio 4)   45

Who killed Billie-Jo (Channel 5)   32

Who wants to be a Millionaire? (ITV1)   137

Who you think I am (BBC4)   121

Whoever Heard of a Black Artist? Britain's Hidden Art History (BBC4)   157

Will Kevin be Home for Christmas? (Aldi)   183

William Blake Singing for England – Omnibus (BBC 4)   33

Witness for the Prosecution (BBC2)   128

Woman's Hour (Radio 4)   64

Women's Euro 2022 Final (BBC1)   114

Wondrous Wales (Channel 4)   33

World Cup 2022 (ITV1)   189

World Cup Match of the Day Live (BBC1)   189

About the Author

David Hallam is a writer and communications specialist who regularly contributes TV, radio and book reviews to the Methodist Recorder and other publications. He serves City Road Methodist Church in Birmingham as a local preacher and in the past has been a borough councillor and a Member of the European Parliament. He and his wife Claire live in Smethwick. They have three grown up children and two adorable grandchildren.

Other Publications

Christabel Pankhurst in Smethwick: the 1918 General Election

Transactions of the Staffordshire Archaeological and Historical Society Volume L · Nov 1, 2018

Taking on the Men: the first women parliamentary candidates 1918

Bewdley, 2018

One hundred years of service to Newton: the history of Newton Road United Reformed (Allen Memorial) Church 1917-2017

Smethwick, 2018

Eliza Asbury, her cottage and her son

Bewdley, 2003.